Reshaping probation and prisons

The new offender management framework

Edited by Mike Hough, Rob Allen and Una Padel

First published in Great Britain in January 2006 by The Policy Press

The Policy Press
University of Bristol
Fourth Floor, Beacon House
Queen's Road
Bristol BS8 1QU
UK

Tel no +44 (0)117 331 4054
Fax no +44 (0)117 331 4093
E-mail tpp-info@bristol.ac.uk
www.policypress.org.uk

© Mike Hough, Rob Allen and Una Padel 2006

ISBN-10 1 86134 812 6
ISBN-13 978 1 86134 812 8

British Library Cataloguing in Publication Data
A catalogue record for this report is available from the British Library.

Library of Congress Cataloging-in-Publication Data
A catalog record for this report has been requested.

Cover design by Qube Design Associates, Bristol
Printed in Great Britain by MPG Books, Bodmin

Contents

Preface

The probation service is approaching its 100th birthday. It has an illustrious past but an uncertain future. Although it is one of the smaller cogs in the criminal justice machine, it is a vital one: it is the one service that intermeshes with all the others. When probation works well it can help bring coherence and direction to the criminal justice system. A malfunctioning probation service can seriously disrupt the wider system.

It is crucial, therefore, that the government's proposals for the National Offender Management Service (NOMS) are shaped in a way that allows the probation service or its successor organisations to thrive.

There is general agreement that reforms of some sort are needed, and needed urgently. The NOMS reforms represent an important opportunity to lay down a proper and durable probation framework. However, the current proposals are thought by most informed commentators outside of government to be high-risk ones. They have been rushed, and often appear to outsiders as only partially thought through. Consultation with key stakeholders has been limited – some would say, perfunctory.

The intention behind this collection of papers is to open up a fuller debate about the organisation of probation work. We hope that politicians, their civil servants, criminal justice managers and others with an interest in justice will all find something of value in the publication.

Mike Hough
Rob Allen
Una Padel

December 2005

Acknowledgements

We would like to thank all those who took part in the symposium recorded through this publication and in particular Martin Narey and his colleagues in the National Offender Management Service for the spirit of openness with which they participated. We are also grateful to Sunita Patel and Sylvia Kusi-Appouh for their help in organising the symposium.

Notes on contributors

Rob Allen is Director of the International Centre for Prison Studies at King's College London. He was previously Director of Rethinking Crime and Punishment at the Esmée Fairbairn Foundation in London, and before that, Director of Research and Development at the National Association for the Care and Resettlement of Offenders (NACRO) and Head of the Juvenile Offender Policy Unit in the UK Home Office. He is a member of the Youth Justice Board for England and Wales. He has extensive experience of international penal reform work, mainly in the field of juveniles and alternatives to prison.

David Faulkner, previously a senior civil servant at the Home Office, is now a senior research associate at the Centre for Criminology, University of Oxford. He teaches and writes on criminal justice and penology. He continues to expose government policy to critical scrutiny in a civilising way. He is heavily involved in the work of many voluntary organisations concerned with law reform. His most recent publication is *Crime, state and citizen: A field full of folk* (2001, second edition in press), an overview of the evolution of criminal policy.

Carol Hedderman is Professor of Criminology at the Department of Criminology, University of Leicester. She was a sentencing and probation specialist in the Home Office for many years. She spent three years at South Bank University as a senior research fellow, returning to the Home Office to lead what is now the NOMS research and statistics team in 2002. She moved to Leicester in 2004. Her research interests include female offenders, the effectiveness of sentencing, reconviction studies and the development of alternative measures of effectiveness.

Mike Hough is Professor of Criminal Policy and Director of the Institute for Criminal Policy Research, King's College London. The Institute has a staff of 15, carrying out policy research for government and independent funders. He has published widely on topics including sentencing and attitudes to punishment, policing, drugs and antisocial behaviour. He was previously Director of the Criminal Policy Research Unit at South Bank University, and before that, Deputy Director of the Home Office Research and Planning Unit.

Alison Liebling is a university reader in criminology at the Institute of Criminology, University of Cambridge. She published her first book, *Suicides in prison*, in 1992. She has continued to conduct a wide range of empirical research in prisons, including key work on the impact of privatisation (*Privatizing prisons: Rhetoric* *and reality,* 1997, with A. James, A.K. Bottomley and E. Clare). Her most recent book is a definitive work: *Prisons and their moral performance: A study of values, quality and prison life* (2004) (Oxford: Clarendon Press).

Mike Maguire is Professor of Criminology and Criminal Justice, School of Social Sciences, Cardiff University. He is shortly to join Glamorgan University on a part-time basis. He has a broad span of research interests, including probation, policing, crime reduction and crime statistics. He is a member of the Correctional Services Accreditation Panel. He is a co-editor of the *Oxford handbook of criminology* (2002), and Senior Academic Advisor to the Crime Reduction Director, Wales. He is also a member of South Wales Probation Board.

Mike Nellis has recently moved to Strathclyde University, where he is Professor of Criminal and Community Justice. He is a former social worker, who has been closely involved in probation training for the last 15 years. He was previously Senior Lecturer in Criminal Justice Studies at the University of Birmingham. He has written extensively on the changing nature of probation, and on community penalties. His current interests include probation organisation, restorative justice and electronic monitoring. His most recent book *Moving probation forward* (2003) (edited with Eric Chui) was published by Longmans.

Una Padel has been Director of the Centre for Crime and Justice Studies at King's College London since 1999. Having been a probation officer in Northumbria Probation Service, Una became Deputy Director of the Prison Reform Trust in 1985. She became Assistant Director of Criminal Justice Projects with Scoda and then coordinator of London Prisons Community Links (LPCL). In June 1998 Una left LPCL to become Director of CLINKS (Prisons Community Links). The function of CLINKS is to develop the role of community-based organisations offering services to prisoners.

John W. Raine is Director of the Graduate School in the School of Public Policy, University of Birmingham. He is a Professor of Management in Criminal Justice and has a long track record of research in this field – specialising particularly on the courts, but more recently on criminal justice policy and management more generally. He has been working with the probation service as teacher and consultant for many years, and is editor of the journal *Vista: Perspectives on Probation, Criminal Justice & Civil Renewal.*

Peter Raynor is Professor of Criminology and Criminal Justice at the University of Wales, Swansea. A former probation officer and former Director of the social work programme in Swansea, his research has included work on the effectiveness of probation and the resettlement of prisoners. His books include *Social work, justice and control* (1985), *Probation as an alternative to custody* (1988), *Effective probation practice* (with David Smith and Maurice Vanstone, 1994), *Understanding community penalties* (with Maurice Vanstone, 2002) and *Rehabilitation, crime and justice* (with Gwen Robinson, 2005) . He is a member of the Correctional Services Accreditation Panel and the Scottish Community Justice Accreditation Panel.

Introduction

Mike Hough

This volume records the proceedings of a symposium that took place in July 2005 on the topic of the National Offender Management Service (NOMS). The event was organised and funded by three centres associated with the School of Law at King's College London: the Centre for Crime and Justice Studies, the Institute for Criminal Policy Research, and the International Centre for Prison Studies.

We decided to mount an event examining the proposals for NOMS because the government had introduced radical proposals for reforming the prison and probation services with limited consultation and with minimal public debate. We decided to focus largely on probation issues because the implications for the probation service were the most immediate and particularly far-reaching. Airing these issues seemed to be of particular value given that although the government was clearly determined on reform, the precise direction of this reform was – in mid 2005 – remarkably unclear. A parliamentary Bill had been introduced in 2004 to make the changes needed to implement the NOMS proposals, but this had yet to pass through Parliament when the 2005 general election was called. At the time of writing (September 2005) it was expected that provisions for NOMS would be included in a Bill to be placed before Parliament in early 2006, transferring statutory responsibility for probation work from probation boards to the Secretary of State. This apart, the content of the Bill remained a matter for speculation.

The symposium was held in Blackfriars, London. Participants included Lord Carter, Martin Narey, the then chief executive of NOMS, and other senior NOMS representatives, as well as academics and representatives of non-governmental organisations with an interest in criminal justice. Coincidentally, Martin Narey announced his resignation as chief executive on the day of the symposium, providing a vivid illustration of the sense of uncertainty surrounding the development of NOMS.

We asked academic experts in the field to prepare six papers to provide the basis of discussion at the event. This volume comprises revised versions of the papers, together with this brief introduction and a final chapter, which aims to capture the flavour of the discussions at the event.

The Carter review and NOMS

In 2002 the government asked Lord Carter to mount a review of the 'correctional services' – that is, the prison and probation services. The review team initially worked under the aegis of the Home Office, although it was subsequently moved to the Prime Minister's Strategy Unit. The report was published in January 2004, in harness with a simultaneous government response (Carter, 2003; Home Office, 2004).[1]

Three central themes run through the Carter report. The first reflects the wider government agenda for 'modernising' the correctional services by deploying a range of strategies associated with the New Public Management. The second relates to the rapid increase in the prison population and ways of bringing this back under control. The third theme is a narrower one, but no less important. It concerns the lack of coordination within corrections: both the lack of coordination between services for offenders under probation supervision, and the poor coordination of resettlement work between prisons and probation.

NOMS, probation and 'modernisation'

In part the Carter report can be seen as the application to the correctional services of New Public Management (NPM) techniques that the government has pursued enthusiastically in other areas of social policy.[2] These include: downward budgetary pressure; the setting of clear priorities and targets for public services; and the introduction of competitive tension into the public sector. Several forms of market system have been tried, including the introduction of purchaser/provider splits (or quasi-markets) within bureaucracies; the introduction of new providers, usually from the private sector, to compete with existing ones; and allowing the consumers of public services greater choice over which providers they use. The concept of market competition as a lever on performance is central to NPM, and the government's current preferred term for it is 'contestability'.

New Public Management emerged in the late 1980s and early 1990s in the UK and US. In its Thatcherite and US manifestations it has tended to be associated with neo-liberal political philosophies about the virtues of small government (see, for example, Wilson, 1989). In the New Labour variant of modernisation, however, NPM is presented not as a retreat from the provision of public services but as a

---

[1] The strategy of simultaneous publication of report and response – with consultation to follow – gives an idea of the sense of urgency for corrections reform within government.

[2] The term New Public Management was coined by Christopher Hood (1991). See McLaughlin et al (2001) for an account of its development within criminal justice in Britain.

change in the way that they are delivered.[3] New Public Management is seen as the best way to drive up public sector performance, and thus improve social justice. It stems from a sense that top-down, monolithic state bureaucracies have actually failed to deliver public services as they were intended. Rather, the argument goes, they have grown into powerful, slow-moving, self-serving bodies with inflexibilities both in their management and their workforces. This critique cannot be lightly dismissed.

The Carter vision of correctional services includes a probation system braced by the tensions of marketplace competition. In his vision the tensions are obviously seen as constructive ones that do not necessarily undermine existing institutions. Precisely how constructive is a question addressed directly or indirectly by several of the chapters in this volume. Mike Nellis (Chapter 5) suggests that the commercial sector will only compete for probation work if it is clear that the market is a substantial one; and that contestability will bring fundamental transformations in work with offenders. His chapter offers a pessimistic prospect of a correctional service from which technology has driven the humanism that has characterised probation's past.

Alison Liebling (Chapter 6) raises some important and subtle points about contestability and organisational values. Traditionalists will appeal to the public service values that are threatened by contestability. Her account of prisons privatisation shows that there can be a dark side to public service work – for example, weak management, workforce complacency and cynicism and union resistance to change – and that private prisons can sometimes outperform public ones in their treatment of prisoners. What is far from clear, however, is that the probation service is currently suffering from a similar malaise as the prison service two decades ago.

Of all the contributions in the book, David Faulkner's chapter (Chapter 7) is perhaps the most optimistic about the gains to be derived from contestability – but he is clear that it needs to be seen as a means of introducing diversity, innovation and experiment, and not as a way of promoting competition for its own sake or simply to drive down costs. His chapter offers a view of a modernised probation system, which fully engages with the government's commitment to localism and to civil renewal – agendas that mesh poorly with the national (or at least) regional dirigisme that infuses NOMS as currently proposed.

---

[3] Some, especially within New Labour, would take issues with the idea that modernisation is a variant of NPM, precisely because of the latter's identification with 'small government', in contrast to modernisation's commitment to social justice.

NOMS and containing the prison population

John Raine's chapter (Chapter 2) considers the interactions between the flexible approach to sentencing that the 2003 Criminal Justice Act introduced and Carter's vision of a more joined-up and constructive approach to offender management. In combination, will they contain the burgeoning prison population? His prognosis veers towards optimism in so far as he sees the reforms as having significant potential in terms of crime reduction, enhanced public confidence and reduced resort to imprisonment. But he offers a gypsy's warning about NOMS' over-focus on issues of 'structures' and 'systems' at the expense of the softer, more subtle, 'processes' and 'commitment' that must support, facilitate and underpin them.

Carol Hedderman (Chapter 4) offers a rather more pessimistic answer to the same question. She sees the flexibility of the new sentencing framework as presenting a significant risk of net-widening. She suggests that sentencers may use their new freedom to assemble incoherent community penalties that are overloaded with conditions; and she points to the consequent burden on the prison that would result from breach proceedings.

Both chapters make the important point that realistic expectations should be placed on community penalties – despite the 'what works' oversell of probation that characterised the late 1990s and early 2000s.

NOMS: seamless supervision of offenders

As several chapters point out, the Carter proposals for better and more seamless supervision of offenders are the least contentious part of his report, and ones that do not necessarily entail the more far-reaching contestability reforms. Existing arrangements for the resettlement of offenders have looked particularly perverse for some time. They involve a form of triage in which probation resources are loaded onto long-term prisoners, many of whom either do not need probation supervision or will not benefit from it. This is at the expense of offenders serving short sentences, who include those most at risk of developing entrenched criminal careers, who probably stand to gain most from effective resettlement.

However, as Peter Raynor and Mike Maguire's chapter (Chapter 3) discusses, considerable progress had been made in addressing these problems in advance of the NOMS proposals. They point out that the organisational changes in the NOMS proposals are not a prerequisite for achieving better case management or for improving a more seamless throughcare 'through the prison gate'. The priority they identify is staff skills development, and the upheaval of large-scale organisational change could actually undermine this. The evolving model of case management reflects both the need to improve case management and the desire to divide up processes for contestability. Raynor and Maguire suggest that the latter should not shape the former.

Questions for NOMS

Those charged with re-engineering the correctional services have to find answers to two key questions. The first is a general one about the overall effectiveness of the modernising toolkits of NPM. This volume addresses this question only at the margins. Those who are sceptical about NPM's general viability will also be sceptical about its application to corrections. However, we can reasonably assume that officials in the Treasury, the Cabinet Office and the Home Office will retain their faith in the value of market solutions for reforming public services in general.

Assuming this to be the case, they need to find answers to the more specific question of whether there are features of probation work that render it less amenable to NPM reforms than other public services. This is a debate that is yet to be had with any clarity.

There are many issues to consider. Here I shall identify the four that strike me as most important ones raised by the chapters in this volume. The first relates to the public as consumers or customers of public services. In a sense, the victims of crime are customers of the criminal justice system; but seen through another lens, the real product of the institutions of justice is compliance with the law, not consumption of its services. An effective criminal justice system commands compliance from all of us; it does not simply provide a service to the 'law-abiding majority', protecting them from the 'criminals'. To work, these institutions need to command authority across the population. It remains an unknown whether elements of the system can be successfully parcelled up into contracts for providers in the private and voluntary sectors without damaging its overall legitimacy.

Second, there are particularly difficult questions about accountability for those public bodies whose role is to deploy the coercive powers of the state. Clearly there is a balance to be struck between local and national accountability, but it may be that systems of contestability tip the balance in the wrong direction. Certainly it is hard to reconcile forms of political accountability at local level with systems of contractual accountability located at regional or national level. There are also potential tensions between providers' accountability to the court and their accountability to the national or regional purchaser. These tensions obviously already exist within the current system, but they could be exacerbated within a framework of contestability.

Third, there remains a complex set of issues about organisational values. It is hard to argue convincingly that the competence and commitment of teachers or doctors in the private sector are compromised by the fact that they work for profit-making or voluntary sector bodies. On the other hand, there may be a greater incompatibility between altruism and the profit motive in those 'helping professions' that involve highly personalised relationships – and relationships into which the 'customer' is coerced. The trust that a good probation officer can command from an offender may be eroded by the latter's realisation that the former is, ultimately, working for shareholders. Similar considerations might apply to the authority and credibility of Pre-Sentence Reports prepared by employees of commercial organisations. If these arguments are sustainable, they might disbar the private sector – but not necessarily the voluntary sector – from some forms of probation work. However, there is a further argument that contestability could compromise the disinterest of providers from all sectors, and not just those in the private sector.

Finally, we do not know whether the provision of correctional services through networks of providers from the statutory, voluntary and private sectors will result in a fragmentation that far outweighs the unifying effects of combining the prison and probation services. Successful probation work may require a sense of joint enterprise, trust between different providers and a commitment to shared goals. To what extent can competition remain friendly and constructive? We do not yet know the answer to this question.

References
Carter, P. (2003) *Managing Offenders, Reducing Crime: A New Approach*, London: Prime Minister's Strategy Unit.

Home Office (2004) *Reducing Crime, Changing Lives*, London: Home Office.

Hood, C. (1991) 'A public management for all seasons', *Public Administration*, vol 69, no 1, pp 3-19.

McLaughlin, E., Muncie, J. and Hughes, G. (2001) 'The permanent revolution: New Labour, New Public Management and the modernisation of criminal justice', *Criminal Justice*, vol 1, no 3, pp 301-17.

Wilson, J.Q. (1989) *Bureaucracy: What Government Agencies Do and Why They Do It*, New York, NY: Basic Books.

2

NOMS and its relationship to crime reduction, public confidence and the new sentencing context

John W. Raine

Introduction

In summer 2005 the prison population in England and Wales reached 77,000 – an all time record – 4,000 higher than in January, and some 30,000 more than a decade earlier. This quite shocking increase has occurred despite the commitment of successive New Labour Home Secretaries since 1997 to promote 'punishment in the community' wherever possible and to make imprisonment a last resort. Concern about the high rate of imprisonment – the highest in Western Europe – has further been heightened in recent times by the similarly shocking statistics on suicides and self-harm in prisons. In 2004 for example, there were 95 suicides in prison, including 13 women, and several thousand incidents of self-harm. Moreover, in one particularly bleak fortnight in June 2005, 12 inmates (of ages ranging from 24 to 64) committed suicide, seven of whom were on remand or awaiting sentence (*The Independent*, 17 June 2005). As the Chief Inspector of Prisons has acknowledged, such tragedies simply cannot be disassociated from the continuing upward trend in the prison population and in the custody rate (in magistrates' courts from 6% to 16% and in the Crown Court from 49% to 60% in the decade to 2003).

This, then, is the depressing background against which this chapter sets out to consider the current and prospective sentencing policy context and its relationship to the proposals for a National Offender Management Service (NOMS). Indeed, arguably the issue of the size of the prison population and the ability of the prison service to be more effective in the challenge of reducing re-offending is the single most important issue in the debate about NOMS and about how success in this respect should be judged (Home Office, 2005a, 2005b; Roberts and Hough, 2005). To date, it would seem that most attention has been focused on structural issues associated with the organisational merger of the two main correctional services

– probation and prisons – with the proposed introduction of 'contestability' and with the organisational arrangements for commissioning and contracting within NOMS (Faulkner and Flaxington, 2004; Faulkner, 2005; Raynor and Maguire, this volume). While in some respects that is perhaps understandable from a staff point of view, it is perhaps of concern that relatively little focus has, as yet, been placed on the process issues that will determine just how effective the new framework can be in meeting the twin targets of crime reduction and enhanced public confidence expected of it.

In this chapter, therefore, we revisit the main features of the new sentencing environment created by the 2003 Criminal Justice Act, the establishment of the Sentencing Guidelines Council and the principle arguments in this regard within the Carter report as a basis for considering how NOMS might work and what its prospects are in the quest for those twin targets of reduced offending and increased public confidence.

The new sentencing context

The starting point for this must be the significant changes in thinking about objectives and principles in sentencing that have emerged in recent years, which have found expression in the 2003 Criminal Justice Act and have subsequently provided the platform upon which the Carter report and the recommendation to establish NOMS have been founded.

The 2003 Criminal Justice Act

The 2003 Criminal Justice Act undoubtedly represents a very significant development in the long-evolving process of sentencing policy and practice – in its way, being quite as significant as the previous milestone legislation of the 1991 Criminal Justice Act. Most important, the new Act, which reflects recommendations in both the Halliday report on sentencing (Halliday, 2001) and the Auld report on the criminal courts (Home Office, 2002), has redefined the purposes of sentencing in ways that generally accord with the policy position that the New Labour government has been advocating for some time:

- The Punishment of Offenders
- The Reduction of Crime (including its reduction by deterrence)
- The Reform and Rehabilitation of Offenders
- The Protection of the Public
- The Making of Reparation by Offenders to Persons Affected by their Offences (2003 Criminal Justice Act, section 142).

At first glance, such aims seem laudably clear. On the other hand, it is not difficult to recognise the scope for tension between some of the five purposes and to envisage some complications in the process of application into practice – most obviously the tension between, on the one hand, 'protecting the public' (for which imprisonment might perhaps be regarded as the appropriate option for serious offenders) and on the other, reform and rehabilitation of offenders (for which the prospects arising from imprisonment are of course very poor) (Ashworth, 2003).

As the recently retired Lord Chief Justice, Lord Woolf, argued in his 2005 Sir Leon Radzinowicz Lecture, the new provisions of the Act '… raise the possibilities of a more focussed role for sentencing. Constructively used, they could increase the public's confidence in community punishment and help achieve a breakthrough in the undue reliance on imprisonment.…'. However, it is clear that there is much to be done if the change to which Lord Woolf and most others aspire is to be brought about.

The 2003 Criminal Justice Act is also a multifaceted and complex piece of legislation that needs to be seen in the context of other legislation from this government – the 2003 Sexual Offences Act, the 2003 Anti-Social Behaviour Act and the 2004 Domestic Violence, Crime and Victims Act (PBA, 2004). Indeed, taken together the various statutes have the potential to drive up custody figures rather than effect the shift to community penalties that ministers wish to see, and there remains at the heart of governmental rhetoric an uncomfortable conflict between, on the one hand, the commitment to get tough on offenders and those who seek to evade their punishment and, on the other, the desire to reduce prison numbers. More generally, after eight years in government, while there is no doubting New Labour's emphasis on being 'tough on crime', there remains something of a question mark about the extent of commitment in reality to the partner component of the 1997 manifesto pledge 'to be tough on the causes of crime' (Roberts and Hough, 2002; Zedner, 2004; Raine, 2005).

The Sentencing Guidelines Council

Among the most important, and probably the more durable, of the provisions of the 2003 Criminal Justice Act has been that to establish a Sentencing Guidelines Council. The primary task of the new Council is to provide authoritative guidelines to the courts on levels of sentencing for different offences and to enable sentencers to make decisions that are supported by better information on the effectiveness of sentences and on the most efficient use of resources. Specifically, the Council is required in Section 170 of the Act to take into account:

- the need to promote consistency in sentencing;
- the sentences imposed by courts to which the guidelines relate;

- the cost of different sentences and their relative effectiveness in preventing re-offending;
- the need to promote public confidence in the criminal justice system.

Three of these four roles – those of 'promoting consistency in sentencing', 'promoting public confidence' and 'monitoring sentencing practices in the courts' probably seem relatively uncontentious. On the other hand, that of 'taking account of the cost-effectiveness of different sentences in drawing up guidelines' is arguably rather more controversial. Here perhaps, judicial purists would take the view that it is for the court alone to decide the just sentence and the responsibility of executive government simply to ensure appropriate capacity in provision. However, that, as Lord Woolf has acknowledged, would be to ignore some of the realities of both sentencing and public finance and to assume '… that there is only one just sentence and unlimited resources, … [when in fact] …criminal justice is in competition with, for example, education and health for resources….' (Woolf, 2005, p14).

The Council is also required to take into account the views of the Sentencing Advisory Panel. This is a body of judges, academics and criminal justice practitioners, as well as public representatives – currently 14 members in total (all appointed by the Lord Chancellor, in consultation with the Secretary of State and the Lord Chief Justice). The Panel predates the Sentencing Guidelines Council to which it now provides its advice, having originally been established in 1999 to provide independent advice to the Court of Appeal, where responsibility had previously lain for issuing new and revised sentencing guidelines (the Magistrates' Association had also been issuing guidance for lay magistrates for a number of years). Before submitting its advice to the Sentencing Guidelines Council, the Advisory Panel is required to undertake wide consultation on its proposals. It does so not just with some 28 statutory consultees but also with reference to a range of other relevant academic and practitioner specialists and by conducting regular open public consultations too.

The Council itself is chaired by the Lord Chief Justice and also comprises seven other judicial members (drawn from every tier of court that deals with sentencing in criminal cases) plus four non-judicial members, but with relevant experience in policing, criminal prosecution, criminal defence and the interests of victims. The chief executive of the new NOMS organisation, although not formally a member of the Council, has also been able to attend and speak at meetings – despite some disquiet on the part of judicial members about the infringement that this is seen to represent to the constitutional doctrine of the separation of powers (by involving an executive government official in what is seen as essentially judicial branch responsibility). Likewise, the chair of the Sentencing Advisory Panel is also invited to attend meetings of the Council to ensure good linkage between the Council and the Panel.

Unlike the previous position pertaining under the Court of Appeal, when guidance had generally been formulated in a reactive manner (that is, in the light of experience from particular cases), the new Sentencing Guidelines Council now takes a proactive stance and does not need to confine its guidelines to any particular offences. Indeed, some of the guidelines already produced have been generic in nature, for example in 2004, one of the first set of guidelines produced related to sentencing discounts for early pleas of guilt. Subsequently the Council has also developed guidelines in relation to the new sentencing provisions of the 2003 Criminal Justice Act to assist in the training of the judiciary, and similarly on the new release provisions for custodial sentences over 12 months, as defined in the Act.

Arguably, the establishment of the new Council and its link with the Sentencing Advisory Panel represents one of the most promising developments in criminal justice practice – bringing a range of expertise, public openness, inclusivity and accountability to a process that hitherto rarely demonstrated such attributes. However, it will be some time before it becomes clear what, if any, impact the Council's work has had in terms of the ambitions for improved public confidence and understanding of the often difficult balancing acts involved in sentencing.

Sentencing and the Carter report

While the focus of the Carter report (2003), was a review of 'correctional services', the analysis and recommendations have picked up strongly on both the changing context and governmental policy on sentencing and on the relation between sentencing practice and the prospects for achieving the desired outcomes of reduced crime and increased public confidence. Carter has summarised the current position in terms of both the poor targeting of sentences and the failure of sanctions to bear down sufficiently on serious, dangerous and highly persistent offenders, the increased use of prison and probation since 1997 for first-time offenders, making poor use of additional investment, and continuing unjustified variance in sentencing practices between areas. Most important, he has argued that:

> The system serves and is driven by the judiciary. However, they do not have sufficient information on the efficacy of different sentences, they are not able to take account of the capacity of the services to deliver the sentences they pass. The result is inconsistent sentences, poor use of resources and continued upward pressure on sentencing – which leads to greater overcrowding and the pressure to release more prisoners through the Home Detention Curfew.... (Carter, 2003, p 20)

The succinct and persuasive vision for sentencing that Carter has offered (and which the government very quickly endorsed in its response [Home Office, 2004]) is of a system in which offenders would indeed be punished for their crimes, the public would be protected, persistent offenders would be punished more severely and face increasing restrictions on their liberty and that offenders would be given the appropriate help to reduce re-offending. His approach has endorsed the intentions of the 2003 Criminal Justice Act to promote greater transparency between the sentence given by the court and that served by the offender and he has emphasised that judges and magistrates will need to be able to discharge their responsibilities for managing demand for probation and prisons to ensure the consistent and cost-effective use of existing capacity. He has also argued that there exists considerable scope for diversion from the courts of low-risk, low-harm adult offenders who plead guilty either through 'final warnings' or by prosecutors deciding instead of court summonses, to ask the offender to pay a fine or make reparations in return for avoidance of a criminal record. Further, he has argued for the replacement of community sentences for low-risk offenders with fines and has advocated the introduction of a 'day fine' system – that is, with the imposition set in day-units of income and with the sanction reinforced by offenders having to face prison for the number of any unpaid days. Again in line with the principles of the 2003 Criminal Justice Act, he has stressed that community sentences should be made more demanding for their target group of medium- and high-risk offenders, and that more extensive use should be made of electronic monitoring. Finally, he has emphasised the importance of both greater sanctions and help for persistent offenders (Ashworth, 2003).

> Persistent offenders need to know that they will be punished more severely.... There needs to be a consistent approach to ensure that the liberty of persistent offenders is progressively restricted.... Strong links need to be forged between prison, probation and other criminal justice agencies ... [with] ... a clear overall approach to managing the offender from bail to resettlement ... [and] ... once identified, persistent offenders should have priority access interventions to help reduce re-offending (in particular, drug treatment).... Custody should be recognised as the ultimate sanction and as such be reserved for the most serious, dangerous and highly persistent offenders.... (Carter, 2003, pp 28-9)

Moreover, in what Carter has described as 'a new role for the judiciary', he has argued for greater emphasis on judicial self-governance, ensuring compliance with guidelines for increased consistency in sentencing practices and better provision of information on individual sentencing practice and its impact on re-offending, with sentencing guidelines in turn informed by evidence of what actually reduces offending and what makes for cost-effective use of existing capacity. He has acknowledged that, in the short term, the capacity of correctional services cannot be significantly increased, given the timescales required to build new prisons and to train probation officers. Accordingly, he has argued, progress initially will need to be made through the pursuit of enhanced consistency through the work of the Sentencing Guidelines Council, the better provision of information and more training and development. To that end, he has suggested that the Sentencing Guidelines Council will need to exercise responsibility for using the existing capacity of correctional services to the best effect, and that the Council will quickly need to develop a comprehensive set of guidelines, having discussed priorities with the Home Office. This in turn, he has suggested, will require a new role for the Sentencing Advisory Panel of independently projecting future demand for prison and probation, of working with the services to produce evidence on the effectiveness of different sentencing options on reducing crime and maintaining public confidence, and of providing judges and magistrates with up-to-date information on their sentencing practices and impacts on re-offending.

Looking further ahead, however, Carter envisages for the medium term a position in which the capacity of correctional services can be changed in terms of scale and composition, to which end, the evidence on efficacy and cost-effectiveness of sentences should inform a dialogue with the Home Office on capacity issues:

> If there were new and convincing evidence on interventions that reduce crime then additional resources would need to be found (for example, if greater use of custody was found to significantly reduce crime, more prisons would need to be built)....
> (Carter, 2003, p 32)

Implementing the new sentencing framework

Among the most persuasive elements of Carter's analysis and his overall portrait for managing offenders is the more systematic relationships that are envisaged between experience of 'what works' in sentencing, the guidance provided by the Sentencing Guidelines Council and the development of practice in sentencing. In many respects, the process envisaged mirrors the ongoing virtuous circle of 'practice, monitoring, learning, reflection and adaptation' frequently discussed in management science circles (see, for example, Senge, 1999). But, of course, putting such good management principles into practice often proves more demanding than anticipated.

Getting sentencing supply and demand in balance

So far as relationships regarding sentencing and the establishment of the NOMS model are concerned, there would seem to be at least three key issues that can be expected to play a part in determining just how well the theory and principles translate into practice and therefore what difference the new framework might make. First, there is a 'supply and demand' issue to be resolved. As Carter has acknowledged, there is very unequal provision of both prison and probation resources around the country which will take time to resolve – valuable time in which impetus and momentum towards realising the goals of better offender management, reduced crime and enhanced public confidence could well be dissipated as other priorities climb the policy agenda. Arguably one of the important steps here will be the development of an infrastructure of suitably equipped local prisons as the means to enable custody and community sentences to work in closer conjunction and to support prisoners maintaining contact with their family networks.

But of no less importance will be the establishment of a much more extensive provision of opportunities for community-based sentences within each locality, enabling sentencers to have all the options at their disposal. Patchy provision for offenders with mental health problems is a particularly acute issue in this context, but there are many other examples besides. Indeed, the inability of the bench to make what is felt to be the most appropriate decision for the offender simply because the facility is unavailable within reasonable travelling distance has long been a source of frustration among the judiciary, particularly magistrates. For instance, in research carried out in 2001, on the enforcement of financial penalties in magistrates' courts (Mackie et al, 2003; Raine et al, 2004), there was widespread support in principle among lay justices for the idea of Attendance Centres as an option for those with unpaid fines (these typically being run by the police and providing a constructive regime of life-skills training on Saturday afternoons). Yet the schemes were only available in a few locations and completely dependent on the goodwill and time-input of individual police officers. With provision of such Attendance Centres being very limited, and in view of the potentially confounding problem of making defaulters incur significant travelling costs to access their nearest such scheme, it was inevitable that the research found very little use made in practice of this well-regarded option. It is important to ensure that the same cannot be said in future of the wider range of community sentences that are promised through the 2003 Criminal Justice Act.

Also particularly important in this regard will be the dialogue and understanding achieved at local level between sentencers and offender managers about the sentencing options available. These days both magistrates and probation officers at local level generally regard the demise of 'Probation Liaison Committees' as having been a particularly regrettable casualty of the introduction of the national probation service in 2000. With hindsight, they now recognise more clearly the potential value of such forums at local level in providing opportunity for exchange and for the growth of better understanding between the bench and the local probation service. While at the time of writing there is little clarity about precisely what and how liaison arrangements at local level are envisaged to operate, it seems essential that a NOMS-equivalent of the Probation Liaison Committees should find its place within the new structure from the outset.

Addressing bench habits and culture

The second key issue likely to be influential in determining just how well the theory and principles of the vision will translate into successful practice in the new framework, concerns the ability of sentencers both to adapt to, and adopt, the full scope of the new sentencing opportunities before them. For lay magistrates in particular, this is likely to be a considerable challenge that will require much more than the typical 'road-show' approach to training. Obviously information provision through training is important, but in addition it will be vital to address the aspects of culture and habit that tend to become characteristic of the way the bench works, particularly panels of lay magistrates. Again, this was an issue that was strongly apparent in the research mentioned above on fine enforcement. There the study found marked variation between courts in the pattern of use of different strategies and sentencing options in response to default. Yet what was also very clear was that the issue was hardly a problem of varying knowledge or awareness – indeed, the samples of magistrates interviewed at all 20 of the courts involved in the research showed strongly consistent awareness of the legal framework for responding to default and of the various options at their disposal. Yet what was also apparent was that at each court a particular culture or habit pattern in sentencing had grown up, which tended to narrow thinking about options in the courtroom and retiring room to a smaller number of regularly deployed approaches.

Moreover, the research noted how such cultures and habits were easily reinforced across the bench because of the rota system that listed the senior (and most influential) magistrates with permutations of more recently appointed members of the bench, who thus learned and began to practice the same habits when their opportunities eventually came for taking the chair in court. The results of such evolving cultures and sentencing habits were very striking indeed. At one court, for example, extensive use was made of the option of Deductions from Benefits, for which the court had developed very good working relations with the local social security office to ensure prompt checking and notification of eligibility for this option. While some magistrates at this court expressed dissatisfaction about the relatively low amount that the rules allowed for such deductions (£2.75 per week at the time of the research) the general view at this particular court was that this was indeed a good strategy for responding to default and one to be used in as many cases as possible (that is, for defaulters in receipt of the appropriate benefits – which in fact was the majority). Yet at another court, not so far away, the practice and reasoning was found to be quite different. Here, magistrates claimed hardly ever to make use of Deductions from Benefits and asserted with equal conviction that this was not a sensible course of action to follow because the procedure was felt to be very bureaucratic and costly to the court in terms of time required to process applications and to deal with the consequences of changes in the benefit status of defaulters (which for many people are quite frequent). Thus, while at both courts, there was similar awareness about the option of Deductions from Benefits as a response to default, very different usage habits and associated justifications for their point of view had developed and shaped their very different practices in the courtroom.

This, then, is a key issue to be confronted if the full possibilities of the new sentencing regime are to be exploited to good effect – for example, the innovation of 'custody plus', of intermittent custody, of the range of requirements that may be attached to a Community Order, the option of unpaid work or of reparation activities, the accredited programmes, the training programmes, the prohibited activity requirements, curfews, exclusion requirements, residence requirements and, as Lord Woolf (2005) has suggested, possibly most important of all, mental health treatment, drug rehabilitation and alcohol treatment requirements. For this array of options to become defined and sustained within the mindsets and habits of each and every court will require tremendous determination and scrutiny of practices by all concerned, and to this end, once again, close liaison between sentencers and offender managers will surely be essential.

Ensuring that 'What Works' really does work

Finally, the third key issue likely to determine how well the theory and principles of the new sentencing climate and the NOMS vision translate into successful practice concerns the 'What Works' approach that has been so strong in the rhetoric of New Labour's approach to public policy including sentencing and criminal justice reform. 'What Works', of course, has seemed a most persuasive and rational approach, purposefully adopted to give legitimacy and scientific objectivity to policy making and practice in this regard (Hood, 2002; Nutley et al, 2003; Robinson, 2005). However, particularly in social policy environments such as criminal justice, there is a real risk of the attribution of spurious legitimacy and objectivity to the very important question of what interventions by practitioners should be followed to reduce offending and re-offending. While a great deal of research has been undertaken over the past eight years, and a great deal has been learned along the way about how and why different responses and interventions work well (and less well) in different situations and for different individuals, the overarching reality remains that still not nearly enough is known. Some of the research has been of questionable design, inadequately prescribed by its commissioners or unduly hurried by the impatience of ministers for results. Moreover, many of the findings from the research have been disappointingly weak or inconclusive in identifying critical factors in cause and effect terms and in predicting risks of re-offending and so on. In some instances, however, the problem has been less with the quality of the research and more a reflection of the reality that offender responsiveness to different sentencing options is extremely unpredictable and indeed that, particularly in relation to persistent offenders, the differences in terms of sentencing outcomes are often very marginal.

All this should not suggest that the research effort has necessarily been in vain. But it does at least signal the need for caution in interpreting and applying many of the findings more widely and in presuming too much of some of the assertions made under the seductive banner of 'What Works'.

The research effort must continue and, with more time available to assess the fuller impacts of different interventions and sentencing options, no doubt better knowledge and understanding will gradually accumulate. But even then, it seems likely that among the most significant determinants of what works well in sentencing terms to reduce re-offending and build public confidence in community penalties will always be the level of human resourcing and scale of commitment devoted to working with offenders and to giving them dedicated personal attention and support towards crime-free ways. Electronic monitoring and other similarly depersonalised surveillance and supervision approaches may have an important role to play in reinforcing other efforts and in helping to keep track of offenders where risks are assessed to be high (Nellis, 2005). But, if the goal is to ensure long-term rehabilitation to crime-free lifestyles, such technological approaches are surely no substitute for the human interaction processes, once known as 'befriending' but now more often referred to as 'mentoring'.

The lesson about the importance of numbers of staff (and consequential profile and visibility) has been learned in recent years in relation to policing, with the government having committed much additional money to the very significant expansion in policing numbers, both of fully trained police constables and the new armies of community support officers who are out and about on the streets. A similar lesson now needs to be learned in terms of expanding staffing levels for probation if the ambitions for reduced re-offending are to be realised and if the prison population is to be steadily brought down in size. Particularly with more police on the streets and therefore more offenders likely to be brought before the courts, and particularly with so much more emphasis now placed on enforcement and sanctions for failure on the part of offenders to comply with the conditions and requirements made of them, it is essential that the management of offenders in the community, within the brave new world of NOMS, involves much stronger provision of personalised support for offenders over the duration of their punishment (MacNeill et al, 2005; Raynor and Maguire, this volume). Lord Woolf has stressed the importance of improving morale and effectiveness of existing probation staff (Woolf, 2005). However, arguably, the greater priority – and one that should in turn help effect an improvement in morale – is to ensure the provision of far more staff and volunteers (whether by 'in-house' provision or by contracts) to enable an altogether more individualised and careful form of support and supervision of offenders than has hitherto been possible.

Conclusion

The combination of the more informed and more flexible approach to sentencing that has now been ushered in by the 2003 Criminal Justice Act and the vision of a more joined-up and constructive approach to offender management that Patrick Carter's review has offered, arguably has the potential to make a very significant difference in terms of crime reduction, enhanced public confidence and, most important, reduced resort to imprisonment and the associated grim statistics with which this chapter opened. However, realisation of that potential depends not just on the hard issues of 'structures' and 'systems' that are put in place but also on the softer, more subtle, 'processes' and 'commitment' that must support, facilitate and underpin them. These softer aspects have been given comparatively little attention in the reports and other published documents so far placed in the public domain. At the time of writing, there is much detail about the NOMS model still to be worked out. As this further detail is developed and elaborated, it seems particularly important that this current imbalance between attention to 'structure' on the one hand and to 'process' on the other is rectified. Otherwise there is a real risk of falling well short of the promising vision of a new and better relationship between the sentencing of offenders and their rehabilitation to better ways under the new NOMS model.

References

Ashworth, A. (2003) *Principles of Criminal Law* (4th edn), Oxford: Oxford University Press.

Carter, P. (2003) *Managing Offenders, Reducing Crime: A New Approach*, London: Prime Minister's Strategy Unit.

Faulkner, D. (2005) 'Relationships, accountability and responsibility in the National Offender Management Service', *Public Money and Management*, vol 25, no 5, pp 299-305.

Faulkner, D. and Flaxington, F. (2004) 'NOMS and civil renewal', *Vista*, vol 9, no 2, pp 90-9.

Halliday, J. (2001) *Making punishments work: Review of the Sentencing Framework for England and Wales*, London: Home Office.

Home Office (2002) Justice For All, Cm 5563, 'The Auld Review', London: Home Office.

Home Office (2004) *Reducing Crime: Changing Lives*, London: Home Office.

Home Office (2005a) *National Offender Management Service, Corporate Plan 2005-06 to 2007-08*, London: Home Office.

Home Office (2005b) *National Offender Management Service, Business Plan 2005-06*, London: Home Office.

Hood, R. (2002) 'Criminal and penal policy: the vital role of empirical research', in A. Bottoms and M. Tonry (eds) *Ideology, Crime and Criminal Justice*, Cullompton: Willan.

Independent, The (2005) Rise in Prison Suicides Blamed on Overcrowding, 17 June (Report by Nigel Morris, Home Affairs Correspondent).

Mackie, A., Raine, J.W., Dunstan, E., Burrows, J. and Hopkins, M. (2003) *Clearing the Debts: The Use and Enforcement of Financial Penalties in Magistrates' Courts*, On-Line Research Report, 10/03, London: Home Office.

McNeill, F., Batchelor, S., Burnett, R. and Knox, J. (2005) *21st Century Social Work: Reducing Re-offending: Key Practice Skills*, Edinburgh: Scottish Executive.

Nellis, M. (2005) 'Out of this world: the advent of the satellite tracking of offenders in England and Wales', *Howard Journal*, vol 44, no 2, pp 125-50.

Nutley, S.M., Davies, H.T.O and Walker, I. (2003) 'Evidence-based policy and practice', *Policy Journal of New Zealand*, vol 20, pp 29-48, June.

PBA (Probation Boards' Association) (2004) *Managing Offenders: Reducing Crime – Changing Lives – the Government's plans for transforming the management of offenders*, Response from the Probation Boards' Association, London: PBA.

Raine, J.W., Dunstan, E. and Mackie, A. (2004) 'Financial penalties: who pays, who doesn't and why not?', *Howard Journal*, vol 43, no 5, pp 518-38.

Raine, J.W. (2005) 'Courts, sentencing and justice in a changing political and managerial context', *Public Money and Management*, vol 25, no 5, pp 290-98.

Roberts, J. and Hough, M. (eds) (2002) *Changing Attitudes to Punishment: Public Opinion, Crime and Justice*, Cullompton: Willan Publishing.

Robinson, G. (2005) 'What Works in offender management?', *Howard Journal*, vol 44, no 3, pp 307-18.

Senge, P. (1999) *The Fifth Discipline: The Art and Practice of the Learning Organisation*, New York, NY: Random House.

Woolf, Lord Justice (2005) 'Making Sense of Sentencing', The Sir Leon Radzinowicz Lecture, Institute of Criminology, Cambridge, 12 May.

Zedner, L. (2004) *Criminal Justice*, Oxford: Oxford University Press.

3

End-to-end or end in tears? Prospects for the effectiveness of the National Offender Management Model

Peter Raynor and Mike Maguire

The concept of 'end-to-end offender management' was fundamental to Patrick (now Lord) Carter's argument for the creation of a new, single agency for the management of prison and community sentences (Home Office, 2003). Now operationalised in the form of the National Offender Management Model (NOMM), it constitutes one of the central planks of the whole 'NOMS enterprise'. Ultimately, indeed, the success or failure of NOMS – in the eyes of practitioners and observers alike – is likely to be judged mainly by the extent to which the new model achieves in practice the key expectations of its designers: in particular, the aims of (a) creating a more holistic and productive experience of sentence management for individual offenders, and (b) contributing demonstrably towards a decrease in reconviction rates.

This chapter discusses elements of the NOMM, and of the organisational context within which it is being introduced, which appear likely to help or hinder the achievement of these aims. In doing so, we draw upon recent theory and research on processes of personal change and desistance from crime, and on effective practice to support such change, especially studies which highlight the importance of practitioner skills, personal relationships and continuity. The first half of the chapter is devoted mainly to discussion of relevant research and of key lessons for policy and practice that have emerged from it: this includes fundamental research on processes of change as well as descriptive and evaluative studies of case management in practice. We then ask to what extent the new arrangements are likely to foster improvements in these areas, concluding that, while the designers of the NOMM aspire to embed many of the principles associated with effective supervision, there are substantial risks that these aspirations will not be realised in practice. They may be disrupted, it will be argued, by a combination of (largely unnecessary) major organisational change and artificial division of functions and processes in preparation for contestability, which may both undermine morale and divert attention from the greater priorities of staff skills development and relational continuity.

Key factors in change processes: practitioner skills, relationships and continuity

Most recent academic literature relating to the reduction of re-offending suggests that processes of personal change (in thinking, attitudes, perceptions of self, and so on) are as important as services to meet offenders' practical needs or to provide opportunities for them to acquire and use skills. Processes of change are emphasised as critical both by advocates of formal offending behaviour programmes and by a quite different group of writers currently developing knowledge and theory about the concept of 'desistance'. For example, the 'What Works' literature, which has underpinned the expansion of cognitive-behavioural programmes in probation and prisons, formulates theories of change built around learning processes in which offenders improve their thinking, self-understanding and motivation as well as their social and practical skills (see, for example, McGuire, 1995,2000; Andrews and Bonta, 2003; moreover, the first criterion for programme accreditation by the Correctional Services Accreditation Panel is that there must be a coherent 'model of change' demonstrating why and how the programme should 'work' – see CSAP, 2004). Again, writers on 'desistance from crime' have produced ample evidence that for many offenders this involves a difficult and lengthy process of change, interrupted by frequent reversals and relapses, which may necessitate the construction of new accounts or 'narratives' about their own identity and their ability to take charge of their own lives rather than remain victims of circumstances (Maruna, 2000; Farrall, 2002; Burnett, 2004).

These broad insights have also directed researchers towards more practical questions about the most effective mechanisms by which offenders can be supported and sustained through the change process. Particular attention has been paid to the potential influence of (a) individual practitioner skills, and (b) continuity (of both relationships and interventions) on the outcomes of supervision. Dowden and Andrews (2004), for example, report on a meta-analysis of the contribution of certain staff skills to the effectiveness of rehabilitative work with offenders. They define these skills as 'Core Correctional Practices' (CCPs), which can be summarised briefly as:

- effective use of authority;
- appropriate modelling and reinforcement;
- the use of a problem-solving approach;
- the development of relationships characterised by openness, warmth, empathy, enthusiasm, directiveness and structure.

The mean effect sizes of programmes were found to be higher when these were present, and significantly higher when other principles of programme effectiveness were also applied: staff skills and programme design complemented each other, rather than one being a substitute for the other. However, the authors point out that:

> Clearly these CCPs were rarely used in the human service programs that were surveyed in this meta-analysis.... These results suggest that the emphasis placed on developing and utilizing appropriate staff techniques has been sorely lacking within correctional treatment programmes. (Dowden and Andrews, 2004, p 209).

In addition, recent literature and practice emphasise two approaches which depend on individual practitioner skills and underpin practice both within and outside 'programmes'. Both are also much more effective where there is time to build up relationships and achieve a degree of continuity. One is pro-social modelling, derived from Trotter's work in Australia (Trotter, 1993); the other is motivational interviewing, derived from the work of Miller and Rollnick (1992) in the field of substance misuse. Both require time and consistency: modelling and reinforcement of pro-social behaviour needs to be consistent and repeated, and motivational interviewing depends on a patient process of helping offenders to see discrepancies between how they behave and what they say they want. Persuading offenders to stick to a plan and to cope with obstacles and difficulties can be easier if the supervisor is involved in the formulation of the plan in the first place; similarly, some offenders will feel a sense of personal obligation to a probation officer whom they see as helpful and reliable, and this is not quickly or easily transferred to a stranger.

The overall message from recent research, then, is that case management (or offender management as it is now called) should aim to reinforce and support offenders' own 'narratives' of change, in addition to helping them to make the best use of available opportunities and interventions, and it is difficult to see how this can be done except in a context of personal communication: that is, in the context of case management as a relational process. Banks apparently know about the importance of a consistent personal link and have developed the concept of the 'personal banker'; similarly most patients like to see their 'own' doctor rather than being allocated to whichever doctor is available on the day (a practice usually justified by telling the patient 'don't worry, they can all access your records on the computer').

Case management in practice: pre-NOMS concerns, initiatives and lessons

Most of the research literature discussed above identifies broad principles which, in an ideal world, would underpin the policies and practices formulated and implemented by agencies that work with offenders, thus enhancing their chances of delivering effective services and reducing reconviction. However, while these ideas were being developed, a different body of research – one aimed primarily at describing and evaluating actual practice – was accumulating evidence of a reality far distant from any such ideal. During the 1990s and early 2000s, a growing number of empirical studies, as well as official reports, identified major weaknesses in case management in both probation and prison practice, most notably a serious lack of continuity between prison sentences and post-release arrangements. In response, evaluated experiments were undertaken (especially by the national probation service) in a search for ways of improving organisational practice. These provided useful further guidance as to the most effective ways of working, some of which influenced work by Tony Grapes and others on what was later to develop into the NOMM. This section outlines some of the relevant research findings and lessons that emerged.

'Through-care' and resettlement

Perhaps the clearest empirical findings in this whole field concerned lack of coordination between what goes on in the prison and what goes on outside. The problems identified included poor liaison during the custodial sentence as well as failure to link post-release services with needs identified or services received in prison. Such studies included substantial reports from the Social Exclusion Unit (SEU, 2002), from the Joint Inspectorates (Home Office, 2001), from voluntary bodies (such as NACRO, 2000), and a series of research studies commissioned by the Home Office to evaluate various approaches to resettlement (Maguire et al, 1996; Maguire et al, 2000; Lewis et al, 2003; Clancy et al, 2006).

The first of this series, carried out 10 years ago, concerned the introduction of Automatic Conditional Release, the first so-called 'seamless sentence', which combined a period in custody and a period under supervision in what was supposed to be a single sentence planned as a coherent whole. It is worth recalling some of the conclusions of that study. Communication between prisons and probation services was generally poor; when it was good, this was because good working relationships already existed between particular prisons and particular teams rather than because people had complied with circulars instructing them to cooperate. Sentence plans were poor and superficial, and were not written to cover the sentence as a whole: at best, prison staff wrote sentence plans about what would happen in prison, and probation staff wrote supervision plans about what would happen in the community. 'Statements about offenders' needs tended to be superficial, or to turn into statements about what courses they wanted to attend, if they were available' (Maguire et al, 1996, p 78).

More recent research on resettlement has concentrated more on the problems of the short-term offenders who represent the majority of prison receptions. This group of prisoners is the least likely to receive programmes or substantial services in prison, and is the most likely to be reconvicted and return to prison. (As one probation manager put it in a memorable mixed metaphor, 'the revolving door can be a downward spiral'.) A study in the mid-1990s showed that probation services, having been encouraged to concentrate on statutory supervision, had largely withdrawn from offering voluntary services to short-term prisoners on release, whatever the prisons or the offenders themselves wanted (Maguire et al, 2000). By the time the Crime Reduction Programme was underway in 1999, this group had been identified as an important target for new initiatives and was the focus of a number of Pathfinder projects designed to provide relevant resettlement services and to increase the motivation of short-term prisoners to cooperate with them.

The results of the first phase of this research, the 'seven Pathfinders' study, have been published and discussed elsewhere (Lewis et al, 2003; Raynor, 2004a). In essence, the projects involved a collaborative approach between the prisons and either local probation services (four projects) or voluntary organisations (three projects). Overall, the probation projects were noticeably more successful in improving offenders' attitudes and reducing their self-reported problems. However, the follow-up study (Clancy et al, 2006) indicates that the critical factor in reducing reconviction may be continuity of contact: after controlling for static risk factors, those who had contact with project workers (either probation officers or trained mentors) after release were significantly less likely to be reconvicted than those who did not.[1]

What is important for current purposes is that continuity of contact seems to have helped to reduce re-offending, and that at least some projects designed to achieve interagency cooperation and an integrated service managed to do so. Broadly speaking, the recent resettlement studies give fairly strong support to the idea that continuity of contact with a helpful service can contribute to helping offenders to stop offending. Together with earlier studies, they also show that collaboration between prisons, probation and voluntary organisations is difficult to achieve, but can be effective. The best continuity seemed to be achieved when contact was maintained with the same people during both custodial and post-release phases: in other words, the best projects provided opportunities for relational continuity.

---

[1] It might of course be argued that the more motivated offenders were more likely both to remain in contact and to desist from offending, so this finding must be treated with some caution. However, it is unlikely that variations in continuity simply reflected differences in motivation among offenders, since different projects achieved very different levels of continuity and indeed participation with what were essentially similar groups of offenders.

Community sentence case management: generic and specialist models

Another significant source for recent thinking about case management has been research on probation practice. Such research offers the important reminder that, whatever the aspirations, being part of the same agency does not in itself guarantee continuity. Ten years ago the evaluation of the STOP programme[2] pointed to uneven follow-up of programme learning by probation officers responsible for supervision after the programme had been completed (Raynor and Vanstone, 1996). Again, in a recent study of probation officers' case management in Manitoba (Bonta et al, 2004), officers were found to be carrying out their risk assessments as instructed, but their supervision plans did not connect with or reflect their risk assessments.

Perhaps the most relevant recent research on case management models is that carried out by Sarah Partridge for the Home Office (Partridge, 2004), which evaluates 'generic', 'specialist' and 'hybrid' models. Generic models link one officer with one offender through a variety of tasks and forms of supervision, from initial pre-sentence report preparation to the end of subsequent supervision or resettlement (this was the standard pattern in most areas until the 1990s: see Burnett, 1996). Specialist models allocate a different officer for different tasks such as report writing, sentence supervision, programme delivery, resettlement, and so on, so that offenders move from officer to officer as they move between teams. This model began in some areas with divisions between 'court teams', 'supervision teams', 'through-care teams' and the like, and was further reinforced by special provision for high-risk cases and by the introduction of programmes as part of the 'What Works' initiative.

Partridge's research concludes that specialist models tend to appeal more to managers than to either practitioners or offenders: they allow managers to be clearer about what resources are being allocated to what functions. Although some practitioners welcomed the opportunity to specialise, particularly in highly skilled tasks, most preferred the generic model. Moreover, offenders clearly wanted continuity of contact with a particular person. They were 'more likely to trust their case manager, address their problems and ask for help if they saw the same person over a period of time' (Partridge, 2004, p 9). Offenders whose supervision was fragmented were confused about what they were supposed to be doing, and did not like having to tell their personal histories to a succession of new officers.

At the same time, it should be noted that the evaluation literature contains plenty of accounts of successful projects that were clearly very specialised. To give a

---

[2] The STOP programme, in Mid-Glamorgan, was one of the earliest offending programmes in Britain based on cognitive-behavioural principles.

few examples, the highly structured West Glamorgan Alternative project of the 1980s worked best when it was operating as a voluntary organisation outside the probation service and receiving offenders from it (Raynor, 1988); the Jersey probation service achieves good compliance and completion rates in a Reasoning and Rehabilitation programme, which is delivered outside the service by further education staff (Miles and Raynor, 2004); and when South Wales officers were required to refer offenders to drugs specialists for assessment, twice as many drug problems were identified and dealt with than when the assessments were left to the probation officers (Raynor and Honess, 1998). Probation staff cannot do everything and should not expect to. However, both the West Glamorgan Alternative and Jersey cases actually illustrate effective continuity in case management: contact with the case managers continued through the programme, and the case managers encouraged compliance, helped with obstacles and motivation, and reinforced the programme learning after it was complete. In other words, relational continuity in case management can coexist with and enhance the impact of specialist interventions. What matters is improving the service, and the effective components of the service are staff skills and the quality of the social processes that occur between individual staff and individual offenders. The test of successful reorganisation will be whether or not it improves these.

So, to sum up this section, continuity matters. From the point of view of offenders, this is most easily understood as continuity of contact with a person they get to know and trust. You do not have to be all working in the same agency to achieve continuity, but it may help; vice versa, continuity is not necessarily achieved even when everyone is within the same agency. Similarly, while continuity may be more likely under generic case management systems, they do not guarantee it, nor is it ruled out by the adoption of a specialist model.

Challenges for **NOMS** and the **NOMM**: getting best value from continuity

We can now consider some of the implications of the above research findings and insights for the proposed NOMS reforms, and particularly for the implementation of the NOMM.

The first thing to say is that the NOMM builds on work by the national probation service that was already in progress prior to the Carter report, and which had begun to take on board some of the key messages about the importance of continuity, increased case management support around interventions, and practitioner skills (especially around motivational interviewing and pro-social modelling). Indeed, to the extent that the new version of the model takes forward these reforms under NOMS, it is clearly to be welcomed. However, there are also a number of serious challenges to be faced, as well as some considerable risks to the achievement of a truly effective system of offender management. These risks and challenges will be discussed under the headings of (a) staff skills, and (b) separation of roles and functions.

(a) Staff skills and officer–offender relationships

Many of the examples described in the above summary of research are drawn from situations where continuity of contact with skilled staff happened to exist and researchers were able to observe the results. To use this information in a systematic way to increase effectiveness would require attention to a number of implementation issues. For example, it is now widely accepted that the dash for programme roll-out to meet targets, which was a feature of the National Probation Directorate's approach to 'What Works', led to a neglect of case management skills and a lack of recognition of the need for skilled supervision outside the programmes. Programmes were used as a substitute for supervision instead of as an enhancement (Raynor, 2004b). A different focus is now needed: not simply on the skills for a selected few to deliver programmes, but on assessing and building practitioner skills across the case manager workforce, and evaluating the impact of doing so. This would require time, patience, care and building on small beginnings, as there is little tradition of working in this way and the appropriate methods and their application would need to be developed. However, this aspect of implementation should not be neglected, as there is little point in promoting continuity of contact with staff who are inappropriately skilled or unhelpful. Staff also need to be guided by the use of relevant, practical and user-friendly assessment systems, and it is arguable that OASys (the national offender assessment instrument) requires further development before it can make a really helpful contribution here.

To engage in a programme of skill development, local innovation and local evaluation is risky for practitioners: they may find many things that need to be improved, and experience of successful innovations in the past suggests that staff need to be motivated by a real curiosity about how to improve services (Raynor and Vanstone, 2001). It is difficult for people to take these risks if morale is low, and difficult for people to feel safe in a context of organisational insecurity. The implementation of restructuring needs to take serious account of this if the aim of restructuring is to enhance effectiveness.

(b) Separation of roles and functions

The NOMM is built around the idea that all offenders will be subject to consistent assessment at the start of their sentences, that this assessment will guide the process of sentence management (both of community sentences and of custodial sentences which continue 'through the gate') and that giving responsibility to a single service will improve effectiveness by ensuring that the plan is followed and implemented. Official descriptions of the model suggest that the process can be effective if it is characterised by the 'four C's of consistency, continuity, commitment and consolidation' (Home Office, 2005, p 6). They also refer repeatedly to offender management as a 'human service process', rather than a bureaucratic, administrative or electronic one. Although they may contain laudable aspirations, these are big assumptions. In the context of major organisational change and staff redeployment, the enforced division in probation areas between those undertaking 'offender management' and those delivering 'interventions', and above all the prospect of further divisions through contestability, doubts must remain whether the vision of a holistic, coordinated 'human service' will be realised, at least in the foreseeable future.

Two examples of potential fragmentation, rather than seamlessness, may be given. The first (and less problematic of the two) is the NOMM's subdivision of offender management itself – ostensibly a 'single concept … and a single… process' (Home Office, 2005, p 4) – into three separate processes of 'management', 'supervision' and 'administration', which may be carried out by one, two or three separate individuals depending on levels of risk, resources and other considerations.[3] Some commentators have argued that there is an inconsistency here, and that a process that is subdivided in this way may not carry the intended message of consistency and continuity to the offender: as Robinson (forthcoming) has recently argued, '"What works" at the level of aggregate "offender management" does not necessarily work for offenders, or indeed the practitioners responsible for supervising them'. The evidence put forward in this chapter suggests that it is important to secure considerable overlap between case management and supervision, and hence that the three-process model may run into difficulties if the two main roles are undertaken by different people. Certainly, there is little evidence in support of the idea that offenders can be successfully managed by people with whom they have minimal human contact. There are also problems associated with the idea of being supervised by somebody who cannot make decisions, and may therefore appear a rather insignificant figure. If the model is really intended to promote relational continuity and appropriate human processes, the three-way division looks artificial.

The second, and potentially much more problematic, risk of fragmentation arises out of the separation of 'offender management' from 'interventions'. This is already being implemented within probation areas, with managers and staff being allocated to one or other 'side' of the organisation (partly in preparation for contestability). While such a separation may appear logical and straightforward on paper, it is already causing practical difficulties for probation areas, which may be experienced

---

[3] It is early days, but the indications are that (except where low-risk offenders are concerned) 'manager' roles will generally be taken by probation officers, while 'supervisor' roles will often be filled by probation service officers.

adversely by offenders. For example, PA Consultancy Group and Mori (2005, pp 33-4) have identified a number of problems in the North-West Region, where the NOMM is being trialled as a Pathfinder. These include major organisational disruption caused by relocation and retraining of staff, staff resistance and role confusions, difficulties in 'unpicking' areas of service delivery where the offender management and interventions were previously integrated within the same role (notably in the case of Drug Treatment and Testing Order teams) and the loss of expert knowledge and networks through the disbanding of specialist teams. The report also notes problems of communication and information sharing, which do not appear to bode well for the future:

> ... historically, probation has struggled to ensure that information about offenders who are attending programmes or undertaking community punishment, is shared in a timely and effective way with programme and CP [Community Punishment] colleagues. This will become a greater challenge in the context of OM [offender management] and interventions split, where OMs will need to be able to monitor the progress of their offenders and their engagement with interventions more rigorously and potentially across a broader range of providers.' (p 33)

Anecdotal evidence and observation in other probation areas identify further problems arising from the split. For example, staff morale appears to be affected in some areas by disquiet among those allocated to 'interventions' who feel vulnerable to contestability. The small numbers of staff in some large rural areas, too, make it difficult to make clear divisions of functions. Another issue is that in areas that had devolved management responsibilities to district level in order to assist the building of networks with other local agencies and communities (a key aim of the government's 'civil renewal' policy), the split of functions has tended to result in a return to head office management of interventions, thus jeopardising the local links.

Disruptive as they are, many of the above problems may turn out to be simply 'teething troubles'. However, in the longer term, perhaps the greatest risk arising from the separation of functions is that both the 'management' of offenders and the delivery of interventions become impersonal processes, while 'supervision' (in the sense of developing relationships with offenders, supporting and motivating them, and so on) falls between the cracks that separate them. The NOMM encourages offender managers, using OASys, to identify a set of specific 'needs' for each offender and to respond to each of these needs by referring the offender to a different specialist service provider (either a probation interventions team or an external provider). For example, 'thinking and attitudes' issues may be addressed by referral to an offending behaviour programme, accommodation needs by referral to a housing agency, and so on. If an offender is spending a considerable amount of time with one or more of the intervention providers, a busy offender manager (who may also be the 'supervisor' in name) may begin to leave support and motivation to those providers. At the same time, the interventions team may see their role purely as providing the specialist service, not as a surrogate supervisor. This problem may be avoided if it is made very clear in job descriptions and formal agreements where responsibilities lie. For example, Holt (2002) distinguishes 'thick' and 'thin' (or 'comprehensive/integrated' and 'administrative/bureaucratic') models of case management, where the 'thick' version includes full personal support and motivational work: a similar distinction could be applied to service delivery, so that, for example, those responsible for drug treatment or programme delivery might agree to provide a 'thicker' form of intervention, which included more support. However, (a) people do not always follow agreements, (b) transferring responsibility for support requires effective communication (which is often not achieved) between offender manager and interventions team about the offender's circumstances, work already undertaken, and so on, and (c) it takes time to build up relationships of trust.

The above problem is not new (see, for example, Kemshall and Canton, 2002, on the reasons for attrition from offending behaviour programmes) and is difficult enough to solve within one agency such as probation where staff tend to know each other well. However, if contestability leads to a much wider range of service deliverers from other agencies (including the private sector), the difficulties around communication and support are likely to multiply. Certainly, the concept put forward under the NOMM of an individual 'offender management team' constructed around each offender – a sort of 'virtual team' consisting of all those contributing to the implementation of the sentence plan – seems highly unrealistic and unlikely to produce a holistic, integrated experience for the offender in the context of contact with several organisations, some in direct competition with each other.

Conclusions

In conclusion, it should first be acknowledged that the NOMM sets out to address some very real and intractable problems, and that several of the key principles to which it aspires – notably those of motivating offenders, supporting personal change and maintaining relational continuity throughout the whole of a sentence – are in accord both with recent messages from research and with the general views of practitioners. It is also important to note that the model was under development well before the advent of the Carter report (2003) and NOMS, and was designed to be implemented within the structure of separate prison and probation services.

However, it is arguable whether it was necessary to the achievement of these aims to create a whole new organisation, to move rapidly towards contestability, or to split 'offender management' from 'interventions' and 'offender managers' from 'supervisors'. A much greater priority, we would argue, was the development of practitioner skills. As the designers of the NOMM have themselves argued, the retention of a 'human service' based around relational continuity is fundamental to the achievement of effective case management and the reduction of re-offending; and as research has amply demonstrated, this depends more on the quality and motivation of staff than the particular organisational structures or case management models within which they work. To raise staff skills and sustain their motivation and morale at a time of major organisational change, and under the shadow of imminent contestability exercises, is a difficult challenge to managers and there is a considerable risk that they will not be successful. Moreover, the somewhat artificial divisions of functions and processes within the NOMM – regarded by many as primarily a preparatory step towards contestability, rather than of clear benefit to work with offenders – may further undermine the aim of producing 'end-to-end' relational continuity. In short, bearing in mind the 'four C's' of consistency, continuity, commitment and consolidation, it is clearly a considerable challenge to try to deliver these through a fifth C of contestability.

References

Andrews, D. and Bonta, J. (2003) *The Psychology of Criminal Conduct* (3rd edn), Cincinnati, OH: Anderson.

Bonta, J., Rugge, T., Sedo, B. and Coles, R. (2004) *Case Management in Manitoba probation*, Ottawa: Public Safety and Emergency Preparedness Canada.

Burnett, R. (1996) *Fitting Supervision to Offenders: Assessment and Allocation Decisions in the Probation Service*, Home Office Research Study 153, London: Home Office.

Burnett, R. (2004) 'To reoffend or not to reoffend? The ambivalence of convicted property offenders', in S. Maruna and R. Immarigeon (eds) *After Crime and Punishment: Pathways to Offender Reintegration*, Cullompton: Willan Publishing, pp 152-80.

Carter, P. (2003) *Managing Offenders, Reducing Crime: A New Approach*, London: Prime Minister's Strategy Unit.

Clancy, A., Hudson, K., Maguire, M., Peake, R., Raynor, P., Vanstone, M. and Kynch, J. (2006: forthcoming) *Getting Out and Staying Out: Results of the Prisoner Resettlement Pathfinders*, Bristol: The Policy Press.

CSAP (2004) The Correctional Services Accreditation Panel Report 2003-4, London: Home Office, www.probation.homeoffice.gov.uk/files/pdf/CSAP_report03to04.pdf

Dowden, C. and Andrews, D. (2004) 'The importance of staff practice in delivering effective correctional treatment: a meta-analysis', *International Journal of Offender Therapy and Comparative Criminology*, vol 48, pp 203-14.

Farrall, S. (2002) *Rethinking What Works with Offenders*, Cullompton: Willan Publishing.

Holt, P. (2002) 'Case management: shaping practice', in D. Ward, J. Scott and M. Lacey (eds) *Probation Working for Justice* (2nd edn), Oxford: Oxford University Press.

Home Office (2001) *Through the Prison Gate: A Joint Thematic Review by HM Inspectorates of Prisons and Probation*, London: Home Office.

Home Office (2005) The NOMS Offender Management Model, London: Home Office, www.noms.homeoffice.gov.uk/downloads/NOMS_Offender_Management_Model.pdf

Kemshall, H. and Canton, R. (2002) *The Effective Management of Programme Attrition*, Leicester: De Montfort University.

Lewis, S., Vennard, J., Maguire, M., Raynor, P., Vanstone, M., Raybould, S. and Rix, A. (2003) *The Resettlement of Short-term Prisoners: An Evaluation of Seven Pathfinders*, RDS Occasional Paper No. 83, London: Home Office.

Maguire, M., Perroud, B. and Raynor, P. (1996) *Automatic Conditional Release: The First Two Years*, Home Office Research Study 156, London: Home Office.

Maguire, M., Raynor, P., Vanstone, M. and Kynch, J. (2000) 'Voluntary after-care and the probation service: a case of diminishing responsibility', *Howard Journal of Criminal Justice*, vol 39, no 3, pp 234-48.

Maruna, S. (2000) *Making Good*, Washington, DC: American Psychological Association.

McGuire, J. (ed) (1995) *What Works: Reducing Reoffending*, Chichester: Wiley.

McGuire, J. (ed) (2002) *Offender Rehabilitation and Treatment*, Chichester: Wiley.

Miles, H. and Raynor, P. (2004) *Community Sentences in Jersey: Risks, Needs and Rehabilitation*, St. Helier: Jersey Probation and After-Care Service.

Miller, W.R. and Rollnick, S. (eds) (1992) *Motivational Interviewing: Preparing People to Change Addictive Behavior*, New York: Guilford Press.

NACRO (National Association for the Care and Resettlement of Offenders) (2000) *The Forgotten Majority: The Resettlement of Short-term Prisoners*, London: NACRO.

PA Consultancy Group and MORI (2005) *Action Research Study of the Implementation of the National Offender Management Model in the North West Pathfinder*, London: Home Office.

Partridge, S. (2004) *Examining Case Management Models for Community Sentences*, Home Office Online Report 17/04, London: Home Office.

Raynor, P. (1988) *Probation as an Alternative to Custody*, Aldershot: Avebury.

Raynor, P. (2004a) 'Opportunity, motivation and change: some findings from research on resettlement', in R. Burnett and C. Roberts (eds) *What Works in Probation and Youth Justice*, Cullompton: Willan Publishing, pp 217-33.

Raynor, P. (2004b) 'Rehabilitative and reintegrative approaches', in A. Bottoms, S. Rex and G. Robinson (eds) *Alternatives to Prison*, Cullompton: Willan Publishing.

Raynor, P. and Honess, T. (1998) *Drug and Alcohol Related Offenders Project: An Evaluation of the West Glamorgan Partnership*, Drugs Prevention Initiative Paper 14, London: Home Office.

Raynor, P. and Vanstone, M. (1996) 'Reasoning and rehabilitation in Britain: the results of the Straight Thinking On Probation (STOP) programme', International *Journal of Offender Therapy and Comparative Criminology*, vol 40, pp 272-84.

Raynor, P. and Vanstone, M. (2001) 'Straight thinking on probation: evidence-based practice and the culture of curiosity' in G. Bernfeld, D. Farrington and A. Leschied (eds) *Offender Rehabilitation in Practice*, Chichester: Wiley.

Robinson, G. (forthcoming) 'What works in offender management?', *Howard Journal*, vol 45.

SEU (Social Exclusion Unit) (2002) *Reducing Re-offending by Ex-prisoners*, London: Office of the Deputy Prime Minister.

Trotter, C. (1993) *The Supervision of Offenders - What Works? A Study Undertaken in Community Based Corrections*, Victoria, Melbourne: Social Work Department, Monash University and Victoria Department of Justice.

4

Keeping a lid on the prison population – will it work?

Carol Hedderman

Between 1993 and 2003, the sentenced male prison population rose by 75% to nearly 56,000. The female sentenced population tripled (to 3,477) over the same period (Home Office, 2004a). The rise, and the overcrowding that has resulted from it, has been deplored by those of a liberal disposition such as the journalist Roger Graef (2001) who believes that prison should be an option of last resort and is, anyway, ineffective in reducing crime. It has been welcomed by those like the head of the right-wing Civitas organisation, David Green (2003), who believes that a rising prison population is a sign of a law-abiding society, that the use of prison is reasonable on retributive grounds alone, but also that crime is falling because prison 'works'. Both sides draw on official statistics and research to support their beliefs, leaving criminal justice practitioners and the wider public free to make up their own minds about whether prison is a justifiable response to offending but confused about whether there is evidence that it is effective.

Others have written eloquently on the moral and philosophical arguments for and against the greater use of imprisonment (compare: Walker, 1991; Hudson, 2003). This chapter deals with this issue from an entirely utilitarian perspective. In other words it leaves aside considerations of whether prison should be used to punish to focus exclusively on whether the increasing use of imprisonment has resulted in any practical benefits. In particular:

- has the increased use of custody helped to increase public confidence in the criminal justice system?
- has it reduced re-offending?
- has it reduced crime?

Evidence is then considered about whether the increased use of custody was driven by crime or was shaped by other factors. Up to this point the chapter shares some common ground with the Patrick Carter's (2003) report on reforming the correctional services and the government's response (Home Office, 2004b). The actions taken as a consequence of those reports – the development of the Sentencing Guidelines Council (SGC), the passing of the 2003 Criminal Justice Act (CJA) and the creation of National Offender Management Service (NOMS) – are then considered in terms of their potential impact on the size of the future prison population. The chapter ends with some thoughts on how some of the risks associated with these developments might be handled to ensure that the prison population does not escalate beyond manageable levels.

Has the rise in the prison population affected public confidence?

For nine consecutive years the British Crime Survey (BCS)[1] has shown that both violent and acquisitive crime have fallen. Overall, crime has fallen by 39% (Dodd et al, 2004). Meanwhile the proportion of the public who thought that crime had increased rose from 59% in 1997 (Mirrlees-Black and Allen, 1998) to 73% in 2002/03 (Dodd et al, 2004).[2] The increased use of custody does seem to have impinged on the public consciousness in so far as, between 1996 and 2001, the proportion who thought that sentencing was too lenient dropped from 51% to 35%. However, over the same period, the proportion who thought that prisons did a good job fell from 38% to 26% (Hough and Roberts, 2004).

Hough and Roberts (2004) also report the results of a MORI telephone survey of 2,689 adults across England and Wales in 2003, which showed that the proportion of the public who thought that prison was effective in keeping offenders secure was twice the size of the proportion who thought it was effective in reforming them (89% and 44%, respectively). This is important as research done for the review of sentencing led by John Halliday (2001) showed that, unprompted, the public regarded stopping offending, reducing crime and creating a safer society as the most important aims of sentencing. The review noted that: 'Very few spontaneously refer to punishment or incapacitation' (Halliday, 2001, p 109). When asked to rank a range of given aims, the public, Justice's clerks, the Crown Prosecution Service, probation officers, solicitors and barristers all ranked rehabilitation first. However, all three types of sentencers (judges, district judges and magistrates) put punishment first – which was only ranked fourth by the public.

---

[1] The BCS is a regularly repeated household survey of victimisation. The Survey is thought to provide a more accurate picture of many forms of crime than police figures as not all crime is reported to the police or recorded by them.

[2] Dodd et al (2004) report that the proportion who thought that crime had increased dropped to 65% in 2003/04. It remains to be seen if this trend will continue (and what will happen to crime).

Given the small increase in belief about sentence severity and the lack of belief in its rehabilitative impact, the increased use of imprisonment does not seem to be justified on the grounds of improved public confidence. Nor does it seem to be fuelled by a public appetite for punishment. While sentencers may believe they are responding to a public demand for 'tougher' sentencing, it seems that this is not what the public immediately think of when asked about sentencing.

Has the rise in the prison population reduced re-offending?

It has been well-established that reconviction rates following different sentences vary largely because of differences in the types of offenders who are given such sentences. Once allowance is made for differences such as offending and sentencing history, age and gender, reconviction rates for most commonly used forms of community supervision and imprisonment vary by only a percentage point or two (see Lloyd et al, 1994; Kershaw and Renshaw, 1997). This is why, when reconviction results are used to measure the impact of the correctional services, statistical modelling is conducted to remove the effect of changes in the case mix they supervise. Recently, such analyses have shown small but steady improvements in the effectiveness of work done by the correctional services (see, for example, Spicer and Glicksman, 2004). Yet the raw (unmodelled) two-year reconviction rates for offenders released from prison rose from 53% in 1993 (Kershaw and Renshaw, 1997) to 61% in 2001 (Home Office, 2004a). Analyses of official statistics (discussed further below) have largely ruled out the possibility that the courts are dealing with more or more serious or more frequent offenders. The modelled reconviction rates show that, if anything, the probation and prison services are being more effective. The most obvious explanation for the rise in raw reconviction rates is that sentencers are employing custody less effectively. If this is correct, the rise in the prison population is not helping to reduce re-offending.

Has the rise in the prison population reduced crime?

There is no direct evidence that the increase in imprisonment has contributed to crime reduction. Carter (2003) quotes some (unpublished) statistical modelling, which suggests that it may have made a small contribution (perhaps 5% of the 39% drop in crime reported by Dodd et al (2004). However, as Carter acknowledged, we still have the one of the highest crime rates among western industrialised countries despite having one of the highest prison populations. Given the unproven crime reductive value of increased imprisonment, and that Carter estimates that the cost of corrections has risen by about £1 billion over the last decade, it is difficult to argue that the increase in the prison population has been either significantly crime reductive or that it has been good value for money.

Carter (2003) does suggest that prison might play a role in combating the activities of the 100,000 persistent offenders who are estimated to commit 50% of all crime. Currently, about 15,000 of these offenders are in prison at any one time. Carter (2003, p 15) suggests that 'If we could identify and incapacitate the 100,000 persistent offenders, crime would fall dramatically'. However, this means:

- holding the 40,000-45,000 (66%-75%) of the current 60,000 prison population who are not 'persistent offenders' is having little impact on crime;
- we need to develop the ability to identify the 100,000 before they become persistent;
- we need to hold them until the risk period is over (perhaps between the ages of 15 to 30). Even this assumes that, offenders stop offending because of age, whereas there is a considerable body of evidence that suggests desistence results from leading a more settled lifestyle, rather than age itself (see, for example, Laub et al, 1998). If this is correct, imprisoning persistent offenders may well extend the risk-of-offending period rather than protecting society during it.

On this basis, it would seem that increasing the use of prison is not likely to be an efficient or effective way of reducing crime for the foreseeable future.

What caused the rise in the sentenced prison population?

Having a negligible effect on public confidence, crime and re-offending might still be acceptable if the increased use of custody simply reflected the courts dealing with more or worse offenders. But the evidence is that they are not (see Millie et al, 2005, for a full discussion). As the Carter (2003) report provides evidence to demonstrate:

- crime has gone down rather than up;
- the numbers coming to court have remained stable;
- offence seriousness has remained stable or fallen;
- more of those sentenced to prison are first-time offenders;
- the proportion with five or more previous convictions has fallen slightly;
- regional variation is not explained by sentencers responding to local problems.

Sentencers have been told this, but their comments in interview studies about the increased use of custody suggest they do not believe it. For example, the judges, district judges and magistrates (especially magistrates) interviewed by Hough et al (2003) were adamant that it was the seriousness of the offending they saw and not their responses that had changed. As Hough et al (2003) and Carter (2003) acknowledge, while centrally held statistics show otherwise, it is possible that there have been some changes in offences that are not picked up in sentencing statistics.

For example, offences that carry the same label over time (for example, actual bodily harm) may have got nastier, possibly because of increases in drug use. There is currently no evidence to support or refute this idea, but it is difficult to believe that so massive a change in the prison population can be the result of differences in offending that are too subtle for the statistics to pick up.

Alternatively, sentencers may be perceiving an increase in drug use while what they are actually seeing is a greater preparedness by both the correctional and health services to deal with drug problems and therefore to count the numbers needing help. It is a common misperception among sentencers, policy makers and researchers that service providers respond to evidence of a problem. Talking directly to those involved in caring for offenders suggests that the opposite is true (Aubrey and Hough, 1997). They see little point in collecting statistics about a problem unless they can help and to do so gives offenders false expectations, which then have to be managed.

Other factors that Carter (2003) acknowledges might have increased the use of custody are: increased maximum sentences; higher entry points in sentencing guidelines; a self-reinforcing discussion between sentencers, the media and politicians about how everything has got much worse; and tougher enforcement. These are all interrelated and their individual effects are hard to measure. They are also largely unaffected by information on effectiveness (with the possible exception of enforcement) but greatly affected by the media clamour for tougher punishment.

Will current plans keep the population to 80,000 by 2010?

The government's overall approach and sentencing philosophy is described in the Carter (2003) report and the then Home Secretary's response (Home Office, 2004b). Key elements include: making sentencing aims explicit and creating new sentences in the CJA 2003 to fulfil them; setting up the SGC and giving it a leading role in ensuring that the spirit of these reforms is adhered to and the new sentences are used as intended; and the creation of NOMS.

It is important to acknowledge that reducing the prison population is not an explicit government objective. Its acknowledged mission is to create a cost-effective and credible sentencing system. Keeping the prison population within affordable bounds (defined as 80,000 by 2010) is expected to result. This is to be accomplished in a number of ways, including:

- improving information to sentencers and improving its credibility by ensuring that it comes from the SGC;
- encouraging low, medium and high-risk offenders to be treated differently using the new sentences created by the CJA 2003;

- diverting low-risk offenders from supervision to less-intensive sentences including fines;
- sentencing medium-risk offenders to one or more community provisions under the umbrella of the new generic community sentence;
- reserving prison for the 'serious, dangerous and highly persistent';
- creating NOMS to provide a seamless prison and community supervision experience for the offender.

These plans have a number of attractions and if they work they could bring the prison population down and have other beneficial effects, such as improving sentencing consistency between courts. However, there are some real challenges to be faced in making them work and it is worth noting in relation to this that the latest projections of the prison population published by the Home Office (2005) suggest that the population may exceed 80,000 by 2010 by more than 11,000.

One of the fundamental problems is that it is not clear whether Carter envisaged prison being reserved for offenders who are serious, dangerous *and* persistent or can be used for the serious, dangerous *or* persistent. It is probably the latter as the new short custodial sentences introduced in the CJA 2003 are unlikely to deter or incapacitate the serious and dangerous. Either definition will (hopefully) see an end to offenders such as first-time shoplifters going in to prison, except of course for breach of a community sentence. However, the vagueness, including the lack of a definition of serious, dangerous or persistent, leaves open the possibility of large numbers of petty repeat offenders being incarcerated.

Another difficulty is the failure to acknowledge that the different aims of sentencing are not necessarily compatible, and may even conflict with each other, in individual cases. Matters might have been more straightforward if the CJA 2003 had brought in a direct correspondence between one sentencing aim and one type of sentence. Instead there has been an increasing tendency to advertise all sentence types as being capable of meeting all sentencing aims. The most obvious example is community service. In renaming it 'community punishment', the government was presumably trying to make its purpose even clearer. The little good this might have done was almost immediately undone by creating 'enhanced community punishment' (ECP), which involves incorporating explicitly rehabilitative elements into the supervision to tackle issues such as poor thinking skills. As Gill McIvor's (1992) research showed, 'old-fashioned' community service did have rehabilitative effects, but that effect was not produced by calling it enhanced and making it look more like probation. She found that a high proportion of offenders felt that they acquired new skills and/or a sense of satisfaction and increased self-confidence from the work they completed. Those who felt most positively about the work were the least likely to be reconvicted. Despite the National Probation Directorate's claim in an edition of their 'Important Information for Sentencers' (Home Office, 2003), ECP is not evidence based. The research, which is said to underlie its introduction (Rex et al, 2004, p 1) concluded that: '… projects focussed on using community punishment work to tackle other offending-related needs did not appear to produce positive outcomes overall'.

Replacing traditional community punishment with ECP may even destroy the rehabilitative effect that community punishment used to have by changing the way offenders experience it. Moreover, if ECP is a little rehabilitative and a little punitive, should sentencers add a short period of probation too or a short period of custody to ensure a proper measure of rehabilitation and punishment? The history of the Combination Order (or Combined Punishment and Rehabilitation Order) shows that the temptation to overload is considerable and it is not obvious how it will be avoided as sentencers decide which of the many parts of 'generic community sentence', introduced by the CJA 2003, to use.

Although sentences might be overloaded if sentencers decide to punish through community punishment, reform through a cognitive-behavioural programme and incapacitate through tagging, this one-to-one match between sentencing aims and sentencing elements has the benefit of being transparent. However, the 'custody plus' sentence introduced under the CJA 2003 is expected to punish, reform and incapacitate. This makes it a dangerously simple option for sentencers, yet the reason it was introduced is not clear. Sentencers have explicitly said on a number of occasions (most recently in Hough et al, 2003) that they do not sentence offenders to custody because of a lack of suitable community alternatives. Rather they consistently say there is no real substitute for custody. The history of introducing alternatives such as community service and combination orders confirms this, as such sentences quickly become alternatives to each other and go down tariff. In 1993 only 19% of community service orders were imposed on offenders with no previous record. By 2003, this had risen to 29%. Over the same period, first-time offenders went from comprising 10% to 16% of those on combination orders (Home Office, 2001, 2004a).

Whether the CJA 2003's reintroduction of unit fines as 'day fines' will ease pressure on the probation service, by diverting less serious offenders (however defined) away from supervision, depends partly on the way it is implemented and partly on how receptive sentencers are to the change. The original scheme, introduced under the 1991 Criminal Justice Act, worked well during piloting in that payment rates increased and imprisonment for default dropped (Moxon et al, 1990). Unfortunately, the scheme, which was implemented nationally, bore little relation to what had been tested in the pilot, in that unit values spanned a far greater range and that all offences were included in the scheme. One or two highly publicised cases, in which offenders who had failed to provide details of their income received high fines for minor offences such as littering, also brought unit fines into disrepute Moxon (1995). There are also signs that at least the lay magistracy does not welcome their reintroduction. Commenting on the Management of Offenders and Sentencing Bill, the Magistrates' Association Sentencing Policy and Practice Committee noted in February 2005:

> The Magistrates' Association expressed strong reservations about the day fines scheme when it was first canvassed, and we see nothing in the proposals in the Bill which make us alter our view.... At a time when so much has been done to improve performance in the collection of fines there can be no justification for a change of this nature. It will cause fresh uncertainty, have a negative effect and in our view, has the same inherent risks as the previous scheme. (www.magistrates-association.org.uk)

Finally, the CJA 2003 is likely to increase the prison population by removing the probation service's discretion in breaching offenders who fail to attend or otherwise comply with supervision on a second occasion. It is obviously important that non-compliance is dealt with firmly as to do otherwise would further reduce public confidence in the criminal justice system. Also, unless offenders actually attend the programmes they have been sentenced to, such programmes will not be effective in reducing offending. While successive versions of the National Standards governing supervision reduced the number of times an offender could fail to attend before breach and (thus) the supervisor's opportunities to cajole or coerce offenders into compliance, they still left the decision to breach in the hands of the probation service. This meant that those who supervised offenders were left with the task of distinguishing the genuinely non-compliant from those whose compliance wavered occasionally. The CJA 2003 not only insists that offenders must be breached on a second failure to comply, but that when they are returned to court, the court should increase the severity of the existing sentence; or revoke the existing sentence and proceed as though sentencing for the original offence. The court is even allowed to impose a custodial sentence of up to 51 weeks where an offender who has not committed an imprisonable offence persistently fails to comply. While this may increase public and sentencer confidence that offenders are not 'getting away with' a failure to comply, this approach will almost certainly result in a significant rise in the numbers being imprisoned for breach. It also reduces the chances that offenders will stay long enough in community programmes to derive any benefit. The danger here is that only those who do not need supervision, because they lead well-regulated lives and are motivated to change, will ever complete (Hedderman, 2003). Those who most need community supervision will quickly go into prison 'by the back door'. As the Prison Reform Trust (2005) has warned, the risk to the prison population of 'custody plus' breach can only be guessed at.

One response to these points may be to argue that these are precisely the sorts of problems the SGC was created to address. It is therefore disappointing that the SGC's advice on this to date simply reminds sentencers that:

> Having decided that a community sentence is commensurate with the seriousness of the offence, the primary objective when sentencing for breach of requirements is to ensure that those requirements are completed. (SGC, 2004a, para 93]

Moreover, the history of sentencing guidelines in other jurisdictions shows clearly that their impact on sentencing is negligible where the guidelines are non-statutory, as they are here (Tonry, 1996, 2004). Also, to date, the SGC has taken an offence-by-offence approach (www.sentencing-guidelines.gov.uk). This makes it harder to detect inconsistencies building up so that, for example, petty persistent offenders may receive more severe sentences than one-off serious offenders. The realism of at least one piece of their advice is also open to question. Operationalising a 15% discount, to allow for longer post-release supervision on custody plus (SGC, 2004b), is going to be a lot harder than working out a 10% or 20% discount.

NOMS

Among the reasons given for bringing the prison and probation services together under NOMS was that '[t]his new structure would break down the silos of the services. It would ensure the end-to-end management of offenders, regardless of whether they were given a custodial or community sentence' (Carter, 2003, p 33). There is no question that the two services have often worked in silos, although it is possible to find examples of good practice (see Fox et al, 2005). But the underlying assumption that a lack of coordination was due to being separate organisations is questionable. That may be part of the reason, but overstretched resources caused by increased caseloads, staff turnover, poor information technology, and even data protection legislation played their part. Overloading both services with new demands to prioritise without ever saying what they should stop doing has also created cynicism and resistance to new ideas (even the good ones!). So while the creation of NOMS may help to provide seamless supervision, it can only do so if these other problems are tackled too.

What can NOMS do?

There seem to be at least five ways in which NOMS can help to ensure that the spirit of the Carter proposals is turned into reality, and also that the prison population is kept within manageable bounds or even reduced. The same actions will also help to keep the probation caseload to manageable levels. Although the increase in the latter is less obvious because it does not involve the expenditure of vast sums on new buildings, there are other hidden costs we should be equally worried about including the safe management of offenders in the community.

The five options are for NOMS to:

- relate rhetoric to reality more closely, starting with compliance and enforcement;

- refine its objectives so that its performance is not tied to the achievement of specific sentencing aims but to a broader, simpler objective like the Youth Justice Board's 'reducing offending';
- rebalance the relationship between sentencers and the probation service to move away from a customer provider model to a partnership model;
- re-establish trust in 'What Works';
- rethink the NOMS information strategy.

Rhetoric and reality

The disjunction between the rhetoric and the reality of what NOMS does is handled carefully by senior managers because they know that resources depend on it and because it prevents politicians tinkering in ways that exacerbate rather than cure problems. One has only to look at the desire to be seen as tough on offenders. This has created such an overzealous enforcement system that it is inhibiting the very thing national standards were originally intended to do, which is to foster compliance. If the breach provisions in the CJA are operationalised, they will undermine effective practice by further limiting what probation officers can do to encourage and insist on compliance. The problem with sensitive handling at the top is that it leaves main-grade staff with two choices. They can exercise discretion and not record incidents of non-compliance, which undermines accountability and creates rather than manages risk; or they can follow the rules, which will divert offenders out of community supervision and into prison before they have had a chance to be made compliant. Ever-toughening enforcement will ultimately lead to supervision being limited to those who do not need it because they are the only ones who never miss an appointment or fail to turn up for their weekend spells of custody.

Getting a closer match between rhetoric and reality is difficult but failing to do so undermines effective practice and goes a long way to explaining poor staff morale and the haemorrhaging of experienced staff from the probation service.

Another example of the rhetoric/reality mismatch is the claim that NOMS will play a significant role in reducing crime. It could do so in theory but for as long as clear-up rates are so low, NOMS will never have much impact on the crime rate. Ultimately claiming something that cannot be achieved will rebound on the service's credibility.

It would also be an aid to public, media, and practitioners' understanding to take a clear stance on proportionality and risk. Given that risk cannot be accurately assessed for individuals with much certainty, advice in court reports on suitable sentences should always be limited by a consideration of proportionality.

Refine objectives

The Youth Justice Board has a single core purpose, which is to 'prevent offending' (www.youth-justice-board.gov.uk/YouthJusticeBoard/). To a degree it has moved the debate away from how that is achieved (that is, inside or outside prison) so it has suffered less from the need to argue that it is punishing, reforming, incapacitating, and so on. If NOMS were to adopt a similar core purpose, and this was accompanied by a return to some simple messages about how these are to be achieved, so much the better. For example: community punishment punishes; short prison sentences punish; longer ones may reform but are only to be used in cases serious enough to justify imprisonment; community sentences are there to assist offenders to become law abiding, but this will not happen overnight. This is not to deny that community punishment or short sentences can reform and that community sentences can tax offenders (although they probably cannot reasonably be claimed to punish in the conventional sense). It is simply saying that other effects may be additional benefits but they are not the reason to use these responses. Simplifying sentencers' choices may help to avoid overloading offenders with so many conditions that failure, breach and custody become virtually inevitable.

Rebalance the relationship between sentencers and the probation service

Arguably, there are some areas of public service where introducing a purchaser/provider split philosophy has achieved some much-needed reform. Indeed Alison Liebling's chapter in this volume (Chapter 6) suggests that the tension injected by privatisation into the prison service was responsible for some improvements in the quality of prisoner treatment. However, the trend to regard sentencers as customers has upset the balance between probation staff and the courts. Increasingly, if probation staff are asked for a view it is on a sentence that the court is already considering. This limits their opportunities to use reports to divert less serious cases from unduly severe penalties. Faced with ever-increasing caseloads, probation managers are reluctant to argue that their staff should be preparing Pre-sentence Reports (PSRs) rather than Specific Sentence Reports as the latter take less time. In my view this has contributed to sentencing drift and is actually creating the excess demand for probation as well as prison resources. Sentencers are certainly consumers of probation services. It is for them to balance decisions in individual cases about whether to prioritise punishment or rehabilitation, but in deciding which sorts of interventions are likely to be effective or ineffective, they need probation advice. NOMS should reverse the trend away from PSRs so that they can give fuller advice on more cases.

The search for new community options to offer sentencers, inspired by the consumerist model, is also unhelpful for two reasons. First, it implies that there is something wrong with existing sentences; and, second, sentencers have themselves said that there are no alternatives to custody as far as they are concerned (Hough et al, 2003). However, there can be more effective ways of reducing offending in specific cases than using custody. That is a message sentencers and the public have sympathy with as the research reported by Halliday (2001), and discussed above, illustrates. Over time, the media may even come to accept this message.

Re-establish trust in 'What Works'

'What Works' has been oversold and rushing to implement a partial understanding of 'What Works' is backfiring. It is important that NOMS goes back to what the evidence says before it's too late. Key changes involve:

- not labelling everything 'What Works'. Calling ECP evidence-based does not make it so and damages the credibility of legitimate claims;
- targeting is central to effectiveness and the ability to target is in its infancy;
- targeting should also be done within a sentencing package that is proportionate. No intervention's rehabilitative impact is so certain that exceeding proportionality can be justified;
- get implementation right. This includes selling the basic concepts to staff. Central initiatives which have taken HQ staff six months to formulate will not be effectively implemented by giving staff a half-day training course.

Re-think NOMS information strategy

Carter calls for better information for sentencers. But sentencers have already been told that it is their behaviour, not that of offenders, which is driving up the prison population. The problem is that most sentencers do not believe it, and some of those who do believe it may not regret it. Sentencers, especially but not exclusively lay justices, do not need more facts. What they need is for trusted sources such as the SGC to draw conclusions from complicated, and sometimes apparently contradictory, research and statistics and to give them a clear steer on what to do; perhaps starting with:

- the overuse of prison is making it less effective;
- protecting the public is more important than punishing offenders. You cannot always do both;
- offenders lead chaotic lives. Sending them to prison because they do not immediately do what they are told on community supervision reduces the chance that we can divert them from crime.

To assume that sentencers would not understand or be prepared to front such positions is to underestimate them. By being fearful about telling sentencers and the public the truth, NOMS is in danger of losing credibility, not safeguarding it.

The regional structure should ensure that these messages can be tailored to local circumstances so that they chime with direct experience.

Overall, there is a realistic prospect that NOMS can take action that will limit both the prison and probation populations but this involves radical repositioning and retrenchment. The question is whether NOMS has the courage to take up the challenge.

References

Aubrey, R. and Hough, M. (1997) *Assessing Offenders' Needs: Assessment Scales for the Probation Service*, Home Office Research Study 166, London: Home Office.

Carter, P. (2003) *Managing Offenders, Reducing Crime: A New Approach*, London: Prime Minister's Strategy Unit.

Dodd, T., Nicholas, S., Povey, D. and Walker, A. (2004) *Crime in England and Wales 2003/4*, Home Office Statistical Bulletin 10/04, London: Home Office.

Graef, R. (2001) 'Prison Does Not Work. We Know That. So Why Do We Send More and More There?',*The Guardian*, 5 February, www.society.guardian.co.uk

Green, D.G. (2003) 'Crime is falling – because prison works', *The Observer*, 20 July, www.observer.guardian.co.uk

Halliday, J. (2001) *Making Punishment Work: Report of a Review of the Sentencing Framework for England and Wales, The Halliday Report*, London: Home Office.

Hedderman, C. (2003) 'Enforcing supervision and encouraging compliance', in W.H. Chui and M. Nellis (eds) *Probation: Theories, Practice and Research*, Harlow: Pearson Education, pp 181-94.

Home Office (2001) *Probation Statistics, England and Wales, 1999*, London: Home Office.

Home Office (2003) *Enhanced Community Punishment: Important Information for Sentencers, Issue 4*, Summer, London: Home Office.

Home Office (2004a) *Offender Management Caseload Statistics, England and Wales, 2003*, Home Office Statistical Bulletin 15/04, London: Home Office.

Home Office (2004b) *Reducing Crime, Changing Lives: The Government's Plans for Transforming the Management of Offenders*, London: Home Office.

Home Office (2005) *Updated and Revised Prison Population Projections 2005-2011, England and Wales*, Home Office Statistical Bulletin 10/05, London: Home Office.

Hough, M. and Roberts, J.V. (2004) *Confidence in Justice: An international review*, London: Institute for Criminal Policy Research.

Hough, M., Jacobson, J. and Millie, A. (2003) *The Decision to Imprison: Sentencing & The Prison Population*, London: Prison Reform Trust.

Hudson, B. (2003) *Understanding Justice: An Introduction to Ideas, Perspectives and Controversies in Modern Penal Theory*, Maidenhead: Open University Press.

Fox, A., Khan, L., Briggs, D., Rees-Jones, N., Thompson, Z. and Owens, J. (2005) Throughcare and Aftercare: Approaches and Promising Practice in Service Delivery for Clients Released from Prison or Leaving Residential Rehabilitation, Online report 01/05, London: Home Office.

Kershaw, C. and Renshaw, G. (1997) *Reconvictions of Prisoners Discharged from Prison in 1993, England and Wales*, Statistical Bulletin 5/97, London: Home Office.

Laub, J.H., Nagin, D.S. and Sampson, R.J. (1998) 'Trajectories of change in criminal offending: good marriages and the desistance process', *American Sociological Review*, vol 63, no 2, pp 225-38.

Lloyd, C., Mair, G. and Hough, M. (1994) *Explaining Reconviction Rates: A Critical Analysis*, Home Office Research Study 136, London: Home Office.

McIvor, G. (1992) *Sentenced to Serve: The operation and Impact of Community Service by Offenders*, Aldershot: Avebury.

Mirrlees-Black, C. and Allen, J (1998) *Concerns about Crime: Findings from the 1998 British Crime Survey*, Findings No. 83, London: Home Office.

Moxon, D., Sutton, M. and Hedderman, C. (1990) *Unit Fines: Experiments in Four Courts*, Research and Planning Unit Paper 59, London: Home Office.

Moxon, D. (1995) 'England abandons unit fines', in M. Tonry and K. Hamilton (eds) *Intermediate Sanctions in Overcrowded Times*, Boston, MA: Northeastern University Press, pp 139-42.

Prison Reform Trust (2005) *Recycling Offenders through Prison*, Briefing Paper, London: Prison Reform Trust.

Rex, S., Gelsthorpe, L., Roberts, C. and Jordan, P. (2004) *What's Promising in Community Service: Implementation of Seven Pathfinder Projects*, Findings 231, London: Home Office.

SGC (Sentencing Guidelines Council) (2004a) *New Sentences: Criminal Justice Act 2003*, London: SGC.

SGC (2004b) *Reduction in Sentence for a Guilty Plea*, London: SGC.

Spicer, K. and Glicksman, A. (2004) Adult Reconviction: Results from the 2001 Cohort, Online report 59/04, London: Home Office.

Tonry, M. (1996) *Sentencing Matters*, New York: Oxford University Press.

Tonry, M. (2004) *Punishment and Politics: Evidence and Emulation in the Making of English Crime Control Policy*, Cullompton: Willan Publishing.

Walker, N. (1991) *Why Punish?*, Oxford: Oxford University Press.

5

NOMS, contestability and the process of technocorrectional innovation

Mike Nellis

Introduction

The ongoing attempt to realise the Carter report's (Carter, 2003; Home Office 2004a) vision of a National Offender Management Service (NOMS) has been fraught with controversy, not least because of the limited consultation with stakeholders affected by the scale, pace and direction of anticipated change, the lack of detail and coherence in the original plan and anxiety about the probable end of the probation service (Probation Board's Association 2004; Napo 2005). Carter's concept of 'contestability' – a mechanism for facilitating greater involvement of the private and voluntary sectors in 'offender management', ostensibly to 'drive up' public sector standards – has caused particular alarm (Rumgay, 2005; Wargent, 2005a, 2005b). Criticism undoubtedly slowed the initiative and exposed its flaws, and after the resignation of its main civil service champion, Martin Narey (in July 2005), the original NOMS project undoubtedly lost momentum, only to be regained some months later.

Nonetheless, two discursive tendencies must still be overcome if a full understanding of NOMS is to develop. The first is the danger of looking at the intended NOMS reforms too narrowly, in a purely probation-centric way, in isolation from the broader and ongoing 'modernisation' of the criminal justice system, as spelled out in Confident Communities in a Secure Britain, the Home Office's Strategic Plan for Criminal Justice 2004-2008 (Home Office, 2004b) and in an earlier document (Home Office, 2001). Modernisation – and possibly 'contestability' – will continue even if NOMS as originally conceived collapses.

The second danger lies in taking the stated view of the NOMSmen – shorthand for the cluster of individuals who devised, developed and set out to implement NOMS – at face value and privileging their views of what is at issue. Greater prescience than other stakeholders or commentators should not be imputed to them simply because they are 'the powerful' (Walford, 1994). Their reading of the times (as

David Garland [2001] astutely describes them, for instance), may be skewed, and – in an era of extreme 'perception management' – their claims about what is desirable and feasible may be at least as partial as anyone else's within the debate.

Technology and crime control

This chapter focuses on contestability, but will carefully qualify the conventional view of what the government wants from it (namely, increased quality, improved standards and cost-savings). It starts from the premise that the present government desires private sector involvement in criminal justice because the private sector does technological innovation – something integral to its modernisation strategy – far better than the public or voluntary sectors. It argues that the Carter report implicitly embodies a belief that the private sector is better equipped and connected, more motivated and more easily incentivised than the public sector to marshal the resources and expertise to deliver new technologies into criminal justice and suggests that one plausible consequence of NOMS-style contestability would be an increase in commercially-derived 'technocorrections' (here understood as a range of surveillant, monitoring, diagnostic and treatment technologies, see Coyle, 2001). This development may or may not raise standards in the sense of doing things more effectively and efficiently (including more cheaply or speedily), but the truly salient point is that technological innovation enables some things to be done differently by creating the possibility of reconfiguring existing organisational structures and processes, and, sometimes, by introducing new products. It is not solely the standards of existing forms and patterns of work that are at issue, but new, or at least augmented, ways of doing that work.

The politically driven emergence of technological innovation in criminal justice is apparent in four sources outside the Carter report: the Home Office Strategic Plan (Home Office, 2004b), the Foresight programme, the 'crime science' movement and the bi-monthly magazine, *Criminal Justice Management*. The Strategic Plan set out five broad policy aims – a neighbourhood focus in policing, a focus on prolific offenders, rebalancing the criminal justice system to convict the guilty and support victims, putting the interests of the law abiding citizen first and harnessing new technology 'to support all of the above and stay ahead of the criminal' (Home Office, 2004b, p 10, emphasis added). The technology referred to included Airwave (a new police communication network, which also facilitates real-time location of all police officers); biometric identity cards; improved DNA databases; better forensics; drug testing; and the use of information and communication technology (ICT) to join up still disparate criminal justice agencies at local and national level into a genuinely integrated system. Second, the Foresight Programme originated in the Department of Trade and Industry in 1993 to identify opportunities and risks posed by new technologies for the commercial world, and was doing the same in the crime prevention field by the late 1990s (Foresight Programme, 1999, 2000). Third, the emerging 'crime science' movement within criminology – in part stimulated by the Foresight Programme (Laycock, 2005) – aims 'to alert, motivate and empower the hard science and engineering community to act as 'scouts' in identifying scientific and technological innovations (STIs) which are relevant to crime [and crime control]' (Ekblom, 2005, p 27).

Lastly, the widely circulating magazine *Criminal Justice Management* (CJM) shows how new technology is already being used to augment criminal justice processes, police work especially, and highlights the connection between technological innovation, management philosophies and private enterprise. Its articles-cum-advertisements indicate that a number of major hardware and software companies – Capgemini, Unisys, British Telecom, Fujitsu, Memex, SunGard – have appointed criminal justice specialists (including hard-headed Futurologists) to do business with key public sector agencies. It offers advice from private sector professionals on how best to engineer cultural change in the public sector, how to work in partnership and how to integrate new technology into an organisation (Jackson, 2004; Parkinson, 2004; Wallis, 2005). Huge emphasis is placed upon the desirability of 'speeding-up' criminal justice processes – and on the ready availability of technologies to accomplish it. In addition, CJM routinely features short descriptive articles on policy developments, showcases politicians and high-profile criminal justice professionals and hosts a prestigious annual London conference. It is suffused with a sense that there is no current problem in the administration of criminal justice that cannot be ameliorated by technology (Kent, 2005).

Despite all this, the prevalence of new (and anticipated) technologies in existing criminal justice agencies has been under-appreciated both by criminologists and by organisations likely to be affected by them – perhaps, especially, the probation service in England and Wales (hereafter, 'in England'). Without this, the significance and implications of 'contestability' are easily misread and oversimplified. Although Garland (2001, p 116) had drawn attention to a 'new infrastructure of computers, information technology and detailed data-gathering [that] had given rise to a new generation of 'smart' crime control, as the police, sentencers and prison authorities began to use computers and geo-coded data to focus-decision making and target interventions' even he, compared to more focused theorists of the ICT revolution (Castells, 2000) underplayed these developments.[1] To be fair, the profound significance of technological changes in criminal justice that have already, 'invisibly', occurred in criminal justice – in official conceptions of offender identity and sentencing – as a corollary of ICT have only recently been made properly visible by Katya Franko Aas (2005a) but, in any case, other technologies – virtual reality, biometrics, developments in neuroscience (better lie detection and drug

---

[1] Key contributions to the technology and crime control debate have been made by Ball et al, 1988; Corbett and Marx, 1992; McCormick, 1994; Susskind, 1996; Ericson and Haggerty, 1997; Norris and Armstrong, 1999; Jones, 2000; Mair, 2000; Chan, 2001; Haggerty and Ericson, 2001; Archambeault, 2002; Gido, 2002; Grau, 2002; McCahill, 2002; Franko Aas, 2004, 2005b; Goold, 2004).

treatments[2], psychopharmacology, gene therapy and artificial intelligence) are also under scrutiny for their crime control potential. Before Franko Aas's book appeared, only Canadian criminologist Kevin Haggerty had really grasped the significance of 'the increasing use of tools and techniques drawn from the physical sciences in the day to day operation of criminal justice':

> The reliance on such technologies and their attendant forms of expertise signals a change in the knowledge structure of the system itself; the routine practices of the police and correctional officers now depend on assorted knowledges and technologies from disciplines that previously had little direct relevance to criminal justice practitioners. (Haggerty, 2004a, p 222)

In England, as elsewhere, it is the police who are, and perhaps always have been, at the forefront of the 'technological revolution' in criminal justice (Ericson and Shearing, 1986; Chan, 2001). Technology has mostly been harnessed for detection and prevention, but as the very term 'technocorrections' suggests, new technological possibilities exist at both ends of the criminal justice process.[3] The original NOMS project, I will argue, in conception at least, was an attempt to facilitate and accelerate technological innovation in criminal justice – to engineer Haggerty's 'change in the knowledge structure of the system itself'. This inevitably cast existing repositories of 'expert knowledge' – the probation service and its associated professional associations, Napo (the probation union) and the Probation Board's Association (PBA – representing local probation employers) – as, at best mere objects of, and at worst obstacles to, the reform process, rather than partners in it.

The concept of 'innovation' permeates this chapter, and requires definition. Perri 6 (1993, p 398) defines it as 'the introduction of changes in the production of goods and services', seeing it 'as part of an overall sequence of change over time', namely

---

[2] Smith (2005, p 22) describes current neuroscientific work that indicates ' that lying is associated with greater brain activity than truth telling and that activity in certain areas of the brain is associated with distinct kinds of lies'. This may yield practical results in the next decade. The Foresight Programme is exploring the potential of technology that alters 'the human body's neurotransmitters, which carry messages around the brain' as an improved means of dealing with drug addiction, one incentive being the £12 billion current annual cost of drug addiction to the country (*The Independent on Sunday*, 10 July, 2005).

[3] The police themselves now operate at both ends of the criminal justice process; both through Multi-Agency Public Protection Arrangements (MAPPA) and joint police– probation prolific offender projects they are already involved in what they call (seemingly independently of the Carter report) 'offender management', with both sentenced offenders and offenders released from prison (Worral and Mawby, 2005). The narrowly focused, probation-centric, NOMS debate appears not have recognised this development (Robinson, 2005). Space precludes detailed comment here, but police-influenced versions of 'offender management' are likely to make significant use of electronic monitoring.

invention (the discovery of new knowledge), innovation (the application of that knowledge) and diffusion (the adoption of that application by others). He then distinguishes three broad types of innovation. Organisational innovation entails changes to the basic structure of the agencies which deliver services, in ways that, broadly speaking, have not been attempted before. It can include the creation of new organisations, the 're-engineering' of a single organisation and the reconfiguring of relationships between organisations, 'thus giving a new market structure to the industry' (6, p 400). Process innovation involves novel alterations to the techniques and procedures for producing or delivering existing goods and services. Product innovation entails the introduction of new types of goods and services, which can either displace or coexist with the older forms – for example, electronic monitoring (of which there will be a specific study below). Organisational, process and product innovation can operate singly or in varying degrees of conjunction. NOMS itself exemplifies organisational innovation, on a potentially grand scale – but implies process and entails product innovation too.

The Roots of NOMS

The perceived need for a Correctional Services Review emerged from the government's synthesis of its various reviews of sentencing, court structures and resettlement strategies, the White Paper 'Justice For All' (Home Office, 2003). The review, briefly under Home Office auspices, was taken over by the Prime Minister's Strategy Unit (which systematically encouraged 'blue skies' thinking by a cluster of policy advisers) and undertaken by healthcare entrepreneur and management consultant Patrick Carter. In retrospect, given the scale and pace of changes it proposed, it can be seen to be the least consultative – the least democratic – of criminal justice reforms in recent years (Padfield, 2004). It resurrected and reworked an idea – the merger of the prison and probation services into a single correctional organisation – that New Labour had canvassed when it was first elected, on the grounds that they were 'silos' whose separateness impeded the possibility of end-to-end management of offenders. This was successfully resisted in 1998, because existing stakeholders and commentators perceived significant and legitimate differences of culture and ethos in the two organisations (Nellis, 1999). Carter largely circumvented the stakeholders, and reconceptualised their work, in a rather anodyne way, as 'offender management'. His review exemplified to an exceptional degree the messianic managerialism – the large-scale, high-speed re-engineering of existing structures and functions to produce 'guaranteed', quantifiable behavioural outcomes – that had come to characterise New Labour's approach to modernisation in general and public services reform in particular (McLaughlin et al, 2001). Thus, over a five year period, a new organisation – NOMS – would weld the prison and probation services into a single administrative entity, which would (in theory) facilitate the 'end-to-end management' of offenders within and across the two agencies (see Hadley, 2005). In addition, mostly at regional level, NOMS would contract out services to the public, private or voluntary sectors by institutionalising 'contestability' – ostensibly a way of discovering the most cost-effective means of reducing offending. While showing some loyalty to the existing, evidence-led, 'What Works' agenda, the review's commitment to 'blues skies' thinking was nowhere more apparent than in its claim that contestability 'would create a strong incentive to try innovative new approaches to managing offenders rather than just *seeing the world through the prism of prison and probation*' (Carter, 2003, p 36; emphasis added) – another way , perhaps, of denoting Haggerty's 'change in the knowledge structure of the system itself'. The review did not specify clearly what it meant by innovation, but it gave strategic prominence to one very obvious recent example of it – electronic monitoring, including the prospect of a startling new variant of it, satellite tracking – a measure that, thus far, had been solely in private sector hands (Nellis, 2005).

An elite group of forward-looking officials within the Home Office – the NOMSmen – have repeatedly portrayed the Carter report as an expression of the government's overarching commitment to continuous improvement of public services. Being 'content with what has already been achieved' (Home Office 2004a, p 9) was not an option: rather 'we now need to go further' (a phrase that occurred twice in the official response to Carter (Home Office, 2004a, p 2 and p 8). Two reasons were given for this. First (and very blandly), the aim was 'to realise the potential of the correctional services'. Second (more specifically), the aim was to 'implement effectively ... the radical new measures set out in the [2003] Criminal Justice Act' (p 9). No attempt was made to explain why 'going further' had to take Carter's particular form , or why – when it was acknowledged to have delivered success – the two-year-old national probation service could not itself continue to take things further. A very superficial logic was apparent in the idea that the seamless sentences associated with the 2003 Act, which emphasised the integration of, and continuity between the custodial and community components of a sentence, required a single agency rather than two separate agencies. It was far from clear, however, that prison and probation had decisively failed to work together on resettlement – indeed existing good practice in this area was acknowledged (Home Office, 2004a, p 10) – or that cooperation between them could not be improved without recourse to something as drastic and disruptive as the NOMS. The ostensible creation of 'seamlessness' in offender management (Hadley, 2005) was, in any case, somewhat contradicted by the simultaneous creation of contestability arrangements, in essence, a split between purchasers and providers in service delivery processes (Home Office, 2004a, pp 10-15).

The rationale of contestability

'Contestability' – the Carter report's chosen term for the mechanism for involving private and not-for-profit sector involvement – originated with the Treasury. Carter proposed that within five years, contestability should be 'introduced across the whole of prisons and community interventions, with outcome-based contracts' (Carter, 2003). The concept – and exactly what it might mean in practice – was and remains ill-defined. At its mildest, contestability seems merely to be a synonym for the process of market testing rather than for the specific outcome of privatisation or contracting out. This is how the Home Office now tends to project it. At its strongest, it seems to be about the engineering of a mixed economy of provision, which intentionally and systematically destroys the near-monopoly of the public sector, in order to institutionalise a permanently competitive – and in the government's terms more desirable – environment. This is what current stakeholders in corrections – the PBA, Napo and the Prison Officers Association (POA) fear is the real agenda, regardless of what is being said officially, even by the HM Inspectorate of Probation (2005, p 5), which ostensibly endorses the mild view.

Either way, contestability involves compelling the public sector to emulate (and indeed improve upon) the alleged cost-effectiveness of commercial organisations if it is to remain involved in service delivery. The Home Office's (2004a, p 14) claim that it is 'not interested in using the private sector for its own sake' and that it simply wants 'the most cost-effective custodial and community sentences no matter who delivers them' is thus somewhat disingenuous. The NOMSmen manifestly do believe that the private sector sets higher standards of efficiency and effectiveness, and that a mixed economy of service provision, with commercial organisations acting as pacesetter, is intrinsically better than a monopoly of state provision. A model of contestability in which commercial organisations were merely used as a threat and an example, and never permitted to become serious contenders for business would never sustain such organisations' interest. In any case, NOMS's model for contestability seems to derive far more from the prison service experience with contracting-out to commercial organisations than from the probation service's experience of 'partnership' with voluntary and community groups:

> The experience of the Prison Service's use of the private sector has been extremely positive…. More significantly, the threat of contestability in running prisons has led to dramatic improvements in regimes and reductions in cost at some of the most difficult public sector prisons. So effective has contestability been, that the public sector have won two prison contracts back from private sector operators, and in the last few weeks, responding to the threat of the private sector, Dartmoor and Liverpool prisons have transformed their performance. We intend therefore to encourage the private and 'not for profit' sectors to compete to manage more prisons and private and voluntary sector organisations to compete to manage offenders in the community (Home Office, 2004a, p 14).

This is a worryingly upbeat assessment of what prison privatisation has accomplished, although as Carter (2002) had already pronounced favourably on this, it is unsurprising. The first independent research into a private prison concluded that it was internal management strategy rather than contracting out per se that improved regimes and standards (Bottomley et al, 1997; James et al, 1997).

One can accept that the privatisation initiative contributed to the undermining of the POA's once baneful attitude towards some progressive policy initiatives, but any rounded analysis of what contracting out has entailed must factor in the drawbacks and difficulties identified by Nathan (2003). He shows that considerations of commercial confidentiality make it difficult to judge whether cost savings have in fact occurred. Contracted-out prisons have also had staffing difficulties, both in terms of competence and retention, and have not had an unalloyed good record of providing purposeful activity and safe environments for prisoners (see Liebling, 2004, pp 116-27 for a sharp analysis of some ethical and empirical issues).

Nathan points out that the initial case for privatising the building and running of prisons in the UK always intended the reduction of costs 'by using *innovative managerial and technological methods* and by concentrating on capital investment rather than increased labour costs' (Adam Smith Institute, 1984; emphasis added). He notes also that in 1996 the representatives of private prison providers indicated to the Home Office that in order to maximise both efficiency gains and opportunities for staff development 'they would like to see between 20 and 25 per cent of the entire prison estate shared among three to five companies' (Nathan, 2003, p 175). Progress towards this figure was slower than the private sector hoped, a fact which, coupled with operational difficulties in private prisons, led Coyle (2003) to conclude that government support for contracting-out was waning. Carter's correctional services report can arguably be seen as an attempt to revitalise this stalling agenda (and, as with the POA in the first round of prison privatisation, may also be understood as an attempt to marginalise the 'obsolete knowledge' represented by Napo and the PBA).

Three companies dominate the private prisons scene in the UK. UK Detention Services was formed in 1987 by the Corrections Corporation of America (CCA) and two British construction companies, McAlpine and Mowlem. Premier Prison Services was formed in 1992 by America's Wackenhut Corrections Corporation and British facilities management company, Serco, and is now – in more variegated form – wholly owned by the latter (and starting to call itself such). Premier has diversified into Premier Custodial Services (running prisons), Premier Monitoring Services (providing electronic monitoring) and Premier Geographix (making electronic monitoring equipment) – as well as being involved in running immigration detention centres. Group 4, a Danish security company, and England's Securicor were multinational corporations with penal interests in many countries before they merged in February 2004 to become Group 4 Securicor. Before their merger, Group 4 had bought Wackenhut, and Securicor had bought Electronic Monitoring Services (EMS) (an American technology manufacturer). The merged company then bought the electronic monitoring component of the American company ADT – although in England it is still using outsourced equipment from Elmotech, an Israeli company. Worldwide, as well as in the UK, the new giant company is now involved in running prisons, prisoner escort services, immigration detention centres, secure treatment centres (for juveniles) and electronic monitoring schemes – as well as retaining their traditional guarding and policing activities. These companies will be serious contenders in any contestability process, as will other similar companies, whose interest has been cultivated by Martin Narey (*The Guardian*, 10 March, 2004).[4] The Home Office's first attempt at market testing/privatising in the post-Carter world – focused on a cluster of three prisons on the Isle of Sheppey – nonetheless foundered when the POA out-manoeuvred them, offering them a performance deal, which forced, at the very least, a postponement of any contracting-out (*The Guardian*, 23 May, 2005).

The NOMS approach to the voluntary (not-for-profit) and community sector (VCS) is largely a development of policy on increasing and strengthening links between probation services and with voluntary agencies that developed in the early 1990s (NOMS, 2005), although it signally fails to learn lessons about what it takes to create 'partnership' that have emerged since then (see Rumgay, 2000). The NOMS policy on the VCS fails to acknowledge the scale and heterogeneity of the sector – the preponderance of small local groups – and fails to appreciate the conditions under which the very qualities for which it is valued – its dynamism, flexibility and dedication – actually flourish. NOMS proposes competitive contracting with the VCS at national and regional levels in ways that automatically favour larger national service-providing organisations and leaves little room for the smaller, local ones to compete. The latter, by dint of their intense commitment to, and investment in, the quality of life in their particular locality, are at least as vital to the civil renewal agenda, which David Faulkner (Faulkner and Flaxington, 2004) has championed so persuasively. The PBA (2005, para 18) criticises NOMS policy towards the VCS as being likely, at worst, to shrink the pool of available local organisations (by starving them of resources) and at best to stifle some of the social innovativeness for which the sector is often feted.

The innovativeness of the voluntary sector can, however, be overstated (and a service can be excellent and essential without necessarily being innovative). Governments since the 1990s have nonetheless tended to exaggerate the innovativeness and flexibility of the VCS simply to weaken the standing of the public sector, although within the VCS both traditionalist and progressive organisations and ideals have always coexisted. VCS innovation has largely been state-funded process innovation – changing the way services are delivered, but rarely altering the services themselves. Victim Support (Rock, 1990) and Circles of Support for released sex offenders (Quaker Peace and Social Witness 2005) are inspiring recent examples of product innovation in the sector, but they are not evidence

---

[4] According to Moses (2004, p 4) two other American businesses are also interested – Cornell Companies Inc, and the euphemistically named Management and Training Corporation (MTC), the latter having had 'links to the running of the infamous Abu Ghraib prison in Iraq'. The link with the US military is confirmed by *The Observer* (24 November, 2004). (See also Prison Reform Trust, 2005.)

in themselves that the public sector can never be innovative. Local government (and local agencies such as probation) can be socially innovative in certain cultural/political circumstances – notably when they are relatively free from meticulous managerial oversight by the centre (Nellis, 1988) – although whether they can be innovative in the ways the government now requires them to be innovative (that is, alert to new technological possibilities) is indeed more arguable.

The existing critique of contestability

Napo has repeatedly highlighted the absence of a proper business case for NOMS, pointing out that improved liaison between prison and probation could be brought about without it, and that injecting greater rationality into sentencing is largely independent of it. Over and above its hostility to punishment-for-profit, Napo was understandably antagonised by the NOMSmen's failure to take probation officers' views into account and by their reckless attitude towards officers' employment status, and towards industrial relations. For Napo, contestability was never merely one among several aspects of the NOMS agenda, but its very heart:

> In our view, the only clear rationale for NOMS, as currently proposed, is the need to restructure the services in order to facilitate one large market and thereby make it easier for the private sector to bid for its work. (McKnight, 2004, p 6)

The PBA and the POA have largely taken the same view, the latter pointing out that 'private sector companies are not going to invest millions of their shareholders money in putting together bids unless they have been given an undertaking of success' (Moses, 2004, p 5). Securicor itself concedes that, as a result of NOMS, 'the UK government is deliberately creating an improved environment in which competition can flourish' (Paterson, 2004, p 7), acknowledging that:

> For the private sector, the changes bring many opportunities, from the provision of security for intermittent custody options – when offenders spend weekdays doing community service and return to prison for the weekend – to the chance to offer innovative, performance-based solutions to the re-offending problem.

Twelve months on, the private sector may itself be growing disillusioned by the apparent chaos into which the NOMS reforms are degenerating, and by the continuing absence of promised mechanisms for achieving contestability (Davies, 2005). Digby Jones (2005), Director-General of the CBI, for example, wrote to the Home Office complaining of its pusillanimity in respect of the failed contracting-out of the Sheppey prisons. Large commercial organisations may still, however, be the long-term beneficiaries of the 'creative destruction' entailed by NOMS. Whether NOMS and contestability as envisaged come to full fruition or not, public sector organisations like the probation service are destabilised merely by remorseless attempts to change them, which serve to prevent the consolidation and perfecting of previous learning, and demoralise experienced staff (Farrow, 2005). Eventually, the only organisations with a capacity to undertake community supervision, after waves of successive reforms have substantially weakened probation, may well be commercial ones like Securicor and Serco (who will take on erstwhile public sector staff to do so).[5] While the HM Inspectorate of Probation (2005, p 5) considers that 'the drive to apply [contestability] to the probation world would continue even in the unlikely event of the whole NOMS concept being dropped' (because it 'emanates directly from the Cabinet Office'), contestability is not the only means by which such organisations can make their presence felt in criminal justice, as the example of electronic monitoring already shows.

Electronic monitoring: whither contestability?

Electronic monitoring (EM) is the most obvious recent example of technologically-based product innovation in criminal justice, which, in England and Wales, if not elsewhere in Europe, is entirely in private sector hands. Since it was rolled out nationally here in 1999, more than 200,000 offenders have been subject to it, mostly using radio frequency technology to monitor curfews, but with some use of voice verification to check variable locations as well. Emulating developments in America, three satellite tracking pilots began in September 2004, the first sustained schemes in Europe.[6] Both the Carter report (2003) and the Home Office Strategic Plan (Home Office, 2004b) portray EM as an unqualified success, something to build on. The latter promised a doubling of numbers of offenders

---

[5] On 26 September, 2004, Securicor placed an advert in *The Observer* newspaper inviting senior staff from probation, mental health, immigration, police and fine enforcement services to become 'Business Advisors', and to 'share your expertise':

As a leading provider of services to the criminal justice system, Securicor Justice Services is already involved in a range of innovative projects. Understandably, we're proud of our performance so far. But we certainly haven't become complacent. We're constantly striving to extend our success, and are looking for people with senior level experience in the Probation, Mental Health, Immigration, Police and Fine Enforcement fields to assist us. Working with our Business Development team you will be involved in a range of activities including helping us to refine our plans, develop our customer networks, and assist with the preparation of commercial bids. You will know your field, be well connected at a senior level, with up to date knowledge of one of the sectors highlighted. Political and commercial awareness are prerequisites.

Eithne Wallis, former Director-General of the National Probation Service, has recently taken a senior management post in Fujitsu Services, promoting the use of new technology in government, including, currently, court services. Her belief that 'technologies can be used actually to *transform* the business of government and bring about a step change in service delivery' (Wallis, 2005, p17; emphasis added) neatly fits the thesis of this chapter.

[6] Bavaria ran a brief, three-month GPS offender-tracking pilot in summer 2004 (personal communication, James Toon, 19 July, 2005).

placed on EM by 2008 – to 18,000. Both documents strongly emphasised the putative virtues of satellite tracking, rendering it emblematic of the wider process of modernisation. In an exclusive interview with Criminal Justice Management, at the time of the Strategic Plan's publication, Paul Goggins, then Minister for Correctional Services, emphasised the momentousness of prospective developments:

> The development of community sentencing will see a great increase in the use of electronic monitoring, both in the traditional curfew role and, through GPS [Global Positioning System] tracking, to set up geo-fencing to enforce exclusion zones. [Goggins said]: 'We want to make greater use of tagging and also to look at the potential of tracking. Tagging can tell you that someone's in a specific place at a specific time but tracking means you can watch them electronically and be where they are as they move around. *We have to open the possibility of tagging to all adult offenders*'. (quoted in Graham, 2004; emphasis added)

The reference to 'all adult offenders' is indicative of how far we have come since the early, selectively targeted EM pilots in 1989/1990 – and of how far we might yet travel. There is a possibility, it seems, that EM could become an integral, normal, commonplace, defining feature of community supervision, rather than, as it tends to have been seen up to now, one item among many in the toolbox available to courts and supervisors. As Securicor observes, commenting on the implications of the 2003 Criminal Justice Act, the likely expansion of EM curfews is a significant business opportunity:

> It is anticipated that the volume of Curfews will increase as sentencers are advised to impose Curfews as a single requirement for offences at the lower tariff of the sentencing scale. Curfews made alongside other requirements shall be for more serious natured offences. An EM Curfew is the least costly option than any other requirement including unpaid work hence Curfews will be increasingly promoted to Sentencers. (Securicor, 2005, p 3)

In England and Wales government interest in EM was triggered in the late 1980s by a private individual outwith the usual network of penal innovation, and pursued as a potentially cost-effective means of toughening community supervision and reducing the use of imprisonment (Nellis, 1991). Security and telecommunication companies Chubb and Marconi were the service providers in the original pilots, with Securicor contracted to provide enforcement. Probation service hostility to the very principle of electronic surveillance was one reason why EM remained in private sector hands (Mair, 2000). A second wave of pilots began in the mid-1990s, which (in 1999), alongside an early release from prison scheme, subsequently became the basis of nationwide provision. Three companies – Securicor, Premier and GSSC – were awarded five-year contracts to deliver EM, the latter (a European subsidiary of an American security company) being bought out by Reliance (a British security company) shortly afterwards. The initial take-up of EM curfews by courts was slow, but has since increased significantly, and expensively. Quite apart from its continuing reservations about surveillance technology, Napo has repeatedly questioned whether EM does provide value for money (for example, Fletcher, 2004). At the time of writing, the National Audit Office was currently investigating this, with a view to reporting in December 2005.

There was never a mixed economy in the provision of EM, nor are there plans to develop one – it is already, it seems, beyond contestability. The Home Office invited new tenders in 2003. Of the seven bodies who bid, only one was a public sector body, which withdrew in the early stages of the process (personal communication, James Toon, 14 June, 2005). The specification for the new contracts explicitly required product innovation – all bidders had to demonstrate a capacity to undertake GPS tracking in anticipation of pilot schemes being established in 2004 (Nellis, 2005). In October 2004 the new contracts went to Group 4 Securicor and Premier, the former company taking over all the south east region from Reliance and some of Premier's former area, giving it 65% of EM provision in England and Wales (Securicor, 2005). Reliance, a much smaller company, lacking its own technology provider, was too small to compete on price with the other two. According to the Electronic Monitoring Team's (now located in the Procurement Section of NOMS) website 'the new contracts represent a saving of about 35% on current volumes and will help the government achieve the 2008 goal of doubling capacity for the EM of offenders' (www.probation.homeoffice.gov.uk, accessed 23 June, 2005).

A case could, in principle, be made for introducing contestability into EM provision, for the public sector to run it, as it does in mainland Europe, and often in the US. Internationally, the English model is anomalous. Elsewhere probation, prison or police departments run EM schemes themselves, buying in the requisite equipment from small technology producers like ElmoTech and On Guard Plus, rather than from huge service providers like Group4 Securicor and Serco, who have ambitious agendas of their own in the criminal justice world. It seems inconceivable now that the English probation service will ever run EM, as it does in Sweden, for example. But, if NOMS-style contestability ever comes in, is it impossible that, in the next round of tendering for EM contracts (in 2010 at the earliest) a technologically savvy, regionalised police force – or a consortium of several – linked to one of the technology producers might be a contender in the bidding process (perhaps using Airwave as the basis of its location monitoring of offenders)? Or is the real lesson here simply that NOMS-style contestability is not always necessary to bring the private sector in – that modernisation can empower and legitimate the sector with or without it (a lesson that can also be drawn from the infusion of technology into the police themselves, the one public sector criminal justice organisation where this has not proved difficult [see McLaughlin and Murji, 2001])?

Conclusion

NOMS has been an expression of 'blue skies' thinking at the heart of government, and an attempt to actualise it. Resistance from stakeholders initially won some concessions, but this now looks at risk of being vanquished. Commercial corrections providers may pull back from contestability if they are not involved on the scale they desire, and only ever used symbolically to threaten the public sector. But while the final shape of NOMSworld will not be exactly as Carter envisaged or Narey hoped, significant change will occur, whose end point cannot yet be ascertained. Government sightlines are unclear, and in any case, open-endedness is being 'designed in'. As a member of the POA executive observes, 'No-one really knows the extent of changes that will occur as the NOMS programme is rolled out' (Gough, 2004, p 20). In its own modernising terms, the government is simply attempting to rip up obsolete and ossified structures and on the rubble of the old and passé, laying the foundation of a fundamentally more flexible, fluid (yet centrally directed) approach to crime control. Creating that responsive, more easily manipulated infrastructure (untrammelled by anachronistic professional interest groups who might stubbornly resist 'progress') is what NOMS-style contestability is mostly all about. Significantly influenced – if not fully dominated – by commercial organisations, the emerging new structures, by design, will never be as stable and enduring as their predecessors;[7] they will be permanently and actively open to organisational, process and product innovation, depending on what becomes available in the global market place and on what elite decision makers deem desirable.

With the publication of Franko Aas's (2005a) Sentencing in the Age of Information, English criminologists can no longer pretend that we are not 'at a historical watershed in terms of our technological response to crime' (Haggerty, 2004b, p 493) and need to factor that insight into their analyses of initiatives like NOMS. Increasingly, in any case, government commitment to technology-assisted modernisation is being openly acknowledged. Initiatives such as ubiquitous CCTV systems and speed cameras, and the proposed imposition of identity cards and of a nationwide road pricing scheme using GPS satellites, for example, make it clear that the present government is indeed intending to bring about significant transformations in the way we live, work and sustain social order. NOMS was

---

[7] At the King's College NOMS colloquium on 1 July, 2005, it was suggested that the architect of NOMS wanted to achieve 'a system that keeps refreshing itself', a structure for offender management that is 'adaptable so it can keep on changing'. It was also suggested that contestability had been seen merely as a mechanism for introducing 'tension' into service provision, and, oddly, that a great deal of privatisation had not been anticipated. Periodic contracting-out to licenced innovators in the commercial world, however, is a plausible strategy for creating the kind of fluid and impermanent structures favoured by NOMS.

conceived as a huge exercise in deliberate detraditionalisation, clearing the ground to allow for the emergence of something new. Whether these changes will bring about the promises that are being used to justify them – mass reduction in crime, and the stabilisation of the prison population – is debatable, although progress could be made – was already being made – towards them without NOMS. Crime control will be reconfigured, transformed, modernised – moulded to better fit the contours of neoliberalism – but whether it will be more or less 'civilised' is open to question. The humanism that unevenly and intermittently leavened (and just occasionally drove) our penal responses throughout the 20th century does not easily co-exist with messianic managerialism.

Whether NOMS is implemented as conceived or not, technological innovation in criminal justice – at the correctional as well as the preventive end of it – will become possible, and not all of it can or should be rejected. Franko Aas's core point is not that all ICT is bad per se, but that we should at least make the effort to appraise how it does change our practices, rather than complacently seeing it as a merely neutral tool. Looking ahead, who, rationally, would oppose outright effective new forms of lie detection and treatment for addiction if their use were subject to proper ethical constraints? Who but the most rabid prisonmongers (or romantic libertarians) would oppose intensive care-and-control packages (with strong EM components) if they were properly targeted, demonstrably crime reductive and sensibly enforced (Roberts, 2004)? Many of the technologies that will make these developments possible are being created and traded in the private sector, but both state and citizen demands for greater security will ensure a market for them independently of (or at least parallel to) any purely commercial 'selling' of them. Such technologies will of course create anxieties (about their reliability) and unease (about their ethics), and will add new costs even while reducing old ones; some might well contribute to a worse world than the one they displace, especially if humanistic values and democratic protocols are circumvented. Small- to medium-sized companies like ElmoTech – whose ambition is only to profit from making smart technology – are surely more manageable (democratically) – than corporations with global ambitions to see 'justice services' privatised.

Deeper deliberation on the advent of 'technocorrections' is surely vital. NOMS-style contestablility is only one mechanism among several for harnessing commercially based technological innovation – as the examples of the police and the EM providers show. While not dwelling on technology, Davies (2005) rightly appreciates the risk of the NOMSmen 'replacing an expensive, ineffective system with a cheaper, equally ineffective one', scouring out existing good practice without being able to guarantee that they are putting something better in its place. Who is to judge the 'something better'? As crime policy makers turn increasingly to technology they will seek support from 'non-criminological forms of expertise' – computer scientists, engineers and biochemists – rather than 'criminologists schooled in the social sciences, [who will be] rendered as passive observers in these important and high-profile decisions about 'what works' in criminal justice'

(Haggerty, 2004a, p 224). To participate constructively in coming debates, criminologists must become more discerning about our technological prospects. Nonetheless, their traditional expertise in policy analysis and their willingness to act as public intellectuals must also be sustained, for someone must still insist, when the situation demands it, that the distance between blue skies and scorched earth is often far narrower than many contemporary modernisers would have us believe.

References

6, P. (1993) 'Innovation by nonprofit organisations: policy and research issues', *Nonprofit Management and Leadership*, vol 3, no 4, pp 397-414.

Adam Smith Institute (1984) *Omega Report on Justice Policy*, London: Adam Smith Institute.

Archambeault, W.G. (2002) 'The impact of computer-based technologies on criminal justice: transition to the twenty first century', in R. Muraskin and A.R. Roberts (eds) *Visions for Change: Crime and Justice in the Twenty First Century* (3rd ed), Upper Saddle River, NJ: Prentice Hall, pp 351-68.

Ball, R.A., Huff, C.R. and Lilly, J.R. (1988) *House Arrest and Correctional Policy: Doing Time at Home*, London: Sage Publications.

Bottomley, K., James, A., Clare, E. and Liebling, A. (1997) *Monitoring and Evaluation of Wolds Remand Prison and Comparison with Public Sector Prisons, in particular HMP Woodhill*, London: Home Office Publications Unit.

Carter, P. (2002) *Review of PFI Market Testing in the Prison Service*, London: Home Office.

Carter, P. (2003) *Managing Offenders, Reducing Crime: A New Approach*, London: Prime Minister's Strategy Unit.

Castells, M. (2000) *The Rise of the Network Society*, Oxford: Blackwell.

Chan, J.B.L. (2001) 'The technological game: how information technology is transforming police practice', *Criminal Justice*, vol 1, no 2, pp 139-59.

Corbett, R. and Marx, G. (1992) 'Emerging technofallacies in the electronic monitoring movement', in J.M. Byrne, A.J. Lurigio and J. Petersilia (eds) *Smart Sentencing: The Emergence of Intermediate Sanctions*, London: Sage Publications.

Coyle, A. (2001) 'Technocorrections – A Vision of the Post-modern Prison', *Prison Service Journal*, no 134, pp 2-4.

Coyle, A. (2003) 'Conclusion', in A. Coyle, A. Campbell and R. Neufeld (eds) *Capitalist Punishment: Prison Privatisation and Human Rights*, London: Zed Books, pp 211-18.

Davies, N. (2005) 'A System in Chaos', *The Guardian*, 23 June.

Ekblom, P. (2005) 'How to police the future: scanning for scientific and technological innovations which generate potential threats and opportunities in crime, policing and crime reduction', in M.J. Smith and N. Tilley (eds) *Crime Science: New Approaches to Preventing and Detecting Crime*, Cullompton: Willan Publishing.

Ericson, R. and Haggerty, K. (1997) *Policing the Risk Society*, Oxford: Clarendon Press, pp 27-55.

Ericson, R. and Shearing, P. (1986) 'The Scientification of Police Work', in G. Bötime and N. Stehr (eds) *The Knowledge Society*, Dordrecht: Reidel, pp 129-59.

Farrow, K. (2005) 'Still committed after all these years? Morale in the modern day probation service', *Probation Journal*, vol 51, no 3, pp 206-20.

Faulkner, D. and Flaxington, F. (2004) 'NOMS and Civil Renewal', *Vista: Perspectives on Probation, Criminal Justice and Civil Renewal*, vol 9, no 2, pp 90-9.

Fletcher, H. (2004) 'The Cost of Tagging', *Napo News*, no 158, p 12.

Foresight Programme (1999) *Just Around the Corner – A Consultative Document*, The Foresight Crime Prevention Panel, London: Department of Trade and Industry.

Foresight Programme (2000) *Turning the Corner*, The Foresight Crime Prevention Panel, London: Department of Trade and Industry.

Franko Aas, K. (2004) 'From narrative to database: technological change and penal culture', *Punishment and Society*, vol 6, no 4, pp 379-93.

Franko Aas, K. (2005a) *Sentencing in the Age of Information: From Faust to MacIntosh*, London: Glasshouse Press.

Franko Aas, K. (2005b) 'The ad and the form: punitiveness and technological culture', in J. Pratt, D. Brown, M. Brown, S. Hallsworth and W. Morrison (eds) *The New Punitiveness: Trends, Theories, Perspectives*, Cullompton: Willan Publishing.

Garland, D. (2001) *The Culture of Control: Crime and Social Order in Contemporary Society*, Cambridge: Cambridge University Presss.

Gido, R.L. (2002) 'The technoeconomic revolution: reengineering criminal justice organisations and workplaces', in R. Muraskin and A.R. Roberts (eds) *Visions for Change: Crime and Justice in the Twenty First Century* (3rd ed), Upper Saddle River, NJ: Prentice Hall, pp 322-30.

Goold, B.J. (2004) *CCTV and Policing: Public Area Surveillance and Police Practices in Britain*, Oxford: Oxford University Press.

Gough, S. (2004) 'Carter and NOMS: the enemy at the door – a critical analysis, Gatelodge – the POA members magazine, December, pp 20-2.

Graham, C. (2004) 'Custody or community: an interview with Paul Goggins', *Criminal Justice Management*, July, pp 4-7.

Grau, J.J. (2002) 'Technology and criminal justice', in R. Muraskin and A.R. Roberts A R (eds) *Visions for Change: Crime and Justice in the Twenty First Century* (3rd ed), Upper Saddle River, NJ: Prentice Hall, pp 305-21.

Hadley, G. (2005) 'Justice end-to-end', *Criminal Justice Management*, May, p 50.

Haggerty, K. (2004a) 'Displaced expertise: three constraints on the policy relevance of criminological thought', *Theoretical Criminology*, vol 8, no 2, pp 211-31.

Haggerty, K. (2004b) 'Technology and crime policy: reply to Michael Jacobson', *Theoretical Criminology*, vol 8, no 4, pp 449-97.

Haggerty, K.D. and Ericson, R.V. (2001) 'The military technostructures of policing', in P.B. Kraska (ed) *Militarizing the American Criminal Justice System: The Changing Roles of the Armed Forces and the Police*, Boston, MA: Northeastern University Press.

HM Inspectorate of Probation (2005) *Annual Report 2004/ 2005*, London: Home Office.

Home Office (2001) *Criminal Justice: The Way Ahead*, Cm 5074, London: The Stationery Office.

Home Office (2003) *Justice For All*, Cm 5563, London: Home Office.

Home Office (2004a) *Reducing Crime, Changing Lives – The Government's Plans for Transforming the Management of Offenders*, London: Home Office.

Home Office (2004b) *Confident Communities in a Secure Britain: The Home Office Strategic Plan 2004-2008*, Cm 6287, London: Home Office.

Jackson, N. (2004) 'Criminal justice – engaging reform', *Criminal Justice Management*, May, p 42.

James, A., Bottomley, K., Liebling, A. and Clare, E. (1997) *Private Prisons: Rhetoric and Reality*, London: Sage Publications.

Jones, D. (2005) Offender Rehabilitation: Business as a Deliverer of Criminal Justice, The 2nd Probation Board's Association Annual Lecture, London: Probation Board's Association.

Jones, R. (2000) 'Digital rule: punishment, control and technology', *Punishment and Society*, vol 2, no 1, pp 5-22.

Kent, S. (2005) 'Future proof', *Criminal Justice Management*, May, pp 12-13.

Laycock, G. (2005) 'Defining crime science', in M.J. Smith and N. Tilley (eds) *Crime Science: New Approaches to Preventing and Detecting Crime*, Cullompton: Willan Publishing, pp 3-24.

Liebling, A. (2004) *Prisons and their Moral Performance: A Study of Values, Quality and Prison Life*, Oxford: Oxford University Press.

McCahill, M. (2002) *The Surveillance Web: The Rise of Visual Surveillance in an English City*, Cullompton: Willan.

McCormick, K.R.E. (1994) 'Prisoners of their own device: computer applications in Canadian criminal justice', in K.R.E. McCormick (ed) *Carceral Contexts: Readings in Control*, Toronto: Canadian Scholars Press, pp 143-54.

McKnight, J. (2004) 'NOMS – a case not proven', *Napo News*, no 136, October, 2004, p 6.

McLaughlin, E., Muncie, J. and Hughes, G. (2001) 'The permanent revolution: New Labour, new public management and the modernisation of criminal justice', *Criminal Justice*, vol 1, no 3, pp 301-18.

McLaughlin, E. and Murji, K. (2001) 'Lost connections and new directions: neo-liberalism, new public managerialism and the 'modernisation' of the British police', in K. Stenson and R.R. Sullivan (eds) *Crime, Risk and Justice: The Politics of Crime Control in Liberal Democracies*, Cullompton: Willan Publishing.

Mair, G. (2000) 'Technology and the future of community penalties', in A.E. Bottoms, L. Gelsthorpe and S. Rex S (eds) *Community Penalties: Change and Challenges*, Cullompton: Willan Publishing.

Moses, C. (2004) 'NOMS is for profit not public service', *Gatelodge – the POA members magazine*, December, pp 4-5.

Napo (National Association of Police Organisations) (2005) National Offender Management Service – April 2005: A Briefing from Napo, London: Napo.

Nathan, S. (2003) 'Prison privatisation in the United Kingdom', in A. Coyle, A. Campbell and R. Neufeld (eds) *Capitalist Punishment: Prison Privatisation and Human Rights*, London: Zed Books, pp 189-201.

Nellis, M. (1988) 'Juvenile justice and the voluntary sector', in R. Matthews (ed) *Privatising Criminal Justice*, London: Sage Publications.

Nellis, M. (1991) 'The electronic monitoring of offenders in England and Wales: recent developments and future prospects', *British Journal of Criminology*, vol 31, no 2, pp 162-85.

Nellis, M. (1999) 'Towards the field of corrections: modernising the probation service in the 1990s', *Social Policy and Administration*, vol 32, no 3, pp 302-23.

Nellis, M. (2005) 'Out of this world': the advent of the satellite tracking of offenders in England and Wales, *Howard Journal*, vol 44, no 2, pp 125-50.

NOMS (National Offender Management Service) (2005) *The Role of the Voluntary and Community Sector in the National Offender Management Service – Strategy for Consultation*, London: NOMS.

Norris, C. and Armstrong, G. (1999) *The Maximum Surveillance Society – The Rise of CCTV*, Oxford: Berg.

Padfield, N. (2004) 'NOMS and Parliament', *Justice of the Peace*, vol 168, 20 March, pp 214-16.

Parkinson, J. (2004) 'Partnering for change', *Criminal Justice Management*, May, p 16.

Paterson, J. (2004) 'The corrections', Access: security issues for business people (a magazine for Securicor customers), Spring, pp 6-7.

PBA (Probation Board's Association) (2004) 'Managing Offenders – Reducing Crime' and 'Reducing Crime – Changing Lives': – The Government's Plans for Transforming the Management of Offenders, Outline response from the Probation Board's Association, London: PBA.

PBA (2005) *The Role of the Voluntary and Community Sector in the National Offender Management Service – Strategy for Consultation*, Response of the Probation Board's Association, London: PBA.

Prison Reform Trust (2005) *Private Punishment: Who Profits?*, London: Prison Reform Trust.

Quaker Peace and Social Witness (2005) *Circles of Support and Accountability in the Thames Valley; the First Three Years – April 2002 to March 2005*, London: Quaker Peace and Social Witness.

Roberts, J.V. (2004) *The Virtual Prison: Community Custody and the Evolution of Imprisonment*, Cambridge: Cambridge University Press.

Robinson, G. (2005) 'What Works in Offender Management?', *Howard Journal*, vol 44, no 3, pp 307-18.

Rock, P. (1990) *Helping Victims of Crime: The Home Office and the Rise of Victim Support in England and Wales*, Oxford: Oxford University Press.

Rumgay, J. (2000) *The Addicted Offender: Developments in British Policy and Practice*, Basingstoke: Palgrave.

Rumgay, J. (2005) 'NOMS bombs?', *Howard Journal*, vol 44, no 2, pp 206-8.

Securicor (2005) 'News item: Criminal Justice Act 2003', Inside Story (the staff newsletter of Securicor Justice Services), no 43, April.

Smith, D.L. (2005) 'Better polygraphs', *Scientific American Mind*, vol 16, no 2, p 22.

Susskind, R. (1996) *The Future of Law: Facing the Challenges of Information Technology*, Oxford: Clarendon Press.

Walford, G. (1994) *Researching the Powerful in Education*, London: UCL Press.

Wallis, E. (2005) 'Intelligent partnering', *Criminal Justice Management*, September, pp 16-17.

Wargent, M. (2005a) 'Contestability: is the model for NOMS fit for purpose?', *Vista*, vol 9, no 3, pp 162-8.

Wargent, M. (2005b) 'Accountability and contestability: justice at any price?', *Vista*, vol 9, no 4, pp 37-42.

Worral, A. and Mawby, R.C.(2005) 'Intensive projects for prolific/persistent offenders', in A.E. Bottoms, S. Rex and G. Robinson (eds) *Alternatives to Prison: Options for an Insecure Society*, Cullompton: Willan Publishing, pp 268-89.

6

Lessons from prison privatisation for probation

Alison Liebling

Introduction: a recap on the introduction of prison privatisation in England and Wales

> The introduction of the private sector into the management of the prison system would certainly represent a bold departure from previous thinking and practice. It offers the prospect of a new kind of partnership between the public and the private sector in this important ... aspect of our national life. We should not be scornful of new ideas which, if successful, will make an important contribution to the government's programme of providing decent conditions for all prisoners at a reasonable cost. (Douglas Hurd, *Hansard*, 1 March, 1989, col. 278)

This chapter considers the experience of the privatisation of prisons in England and Wales, and draws out some of the implications of this experience for the probation service as they face contestability, or competition from alternative providers of services they have traditionally delivered. The motives for, and context of, this phase of competition over who might provide 'criminal justice services' are somewhat different, so direct extrapolation would be a mistake. However, there is much to be learned from reflecting on prison privatisation thus far.

The first private prison to open in England since prisons were nationalised in 1877 was Wolds Remand Prison. It opened in April 1992, following the 1991 Criminal Justice Act, which authorised the contracting out of any prison to the private sector. One of the aims of this 'experiment' was to establish whether the private sector could play a role in securing improvements to conditions for prisoners, particularly those on remand (House of Commons, 1987, para 15; Home Office, 1988, para 100). It is important to remember the context in which this decision was made: the public sector was under serious scrutiny in several respects, and in prisons in particular, there were major problems of overcrowding, staff unrest, prisoner disturbances and ineffective management (King and McDermott, 1989). Not all of these problems have been completely solved (Home Office, 2000), so for example, it is still the case that some staff in some public sector prisons delay unlocking prisoners, lock them up early, cancel exercise at the drop of a hat, and treat prisoners with a studied indifference that is quite damaging. There has, however, been considerable improvement over the last decade: so for example, generally, impoverished regimes come to light, 'failing prisons' are targeted for improvement, and regime standards have improved in local, as well as, other prisons.

There are now 11 private prisons, managed by four companies: Premier Prison Services (Ashfield, Doncaster, Dovegate, Lowdham Grange), Global Solutions Ltd (Altcourse, Rye Hill, Wolds), Securicor (Parc), and UK Detention Services (Bronzefield, Forest Bank, Peterborough). Two formerly privately managed prisons have been returned to the public sector following competition (Blakenhurst and Buckley Hall). The public sector has been successful in all the performance improvement programmes conducted without competition (but with the threat reserved for a later stage) to date.

The most recently opened private prison is Peterborough, an 840-place mixed prison holding 480 male and 360 female prisoners, operated by UK Detention Services. It opened in April 2005, and was due to reach maximum capacity by August 2005.

All private prisons in England and Wales are directed by ex-prison service governors. Ninety-five per cent of the ground level staff are recruited by the companies involved, are trained locally, and have no prior prison experience. There is a higher turnover of staff in private prisons than in public sector prisons, including a small but significant drift from private to public sector prison employment, where pay and conditions are better.

The public, including reasonably well-informed law undergraduates, have very little knowledge on this subject, and often express surprise that we have private prisons at all. There has been one independent evaluation of any private prison in this country (Bottomley et al, 1997; James et al, 1997), although there have been several official cost and quality comparisons (for example, Woodbridge, 1999; Park, 2000) and many studies in other jurisdictions (for example, Moyle, 1995, 2001; Camp and Gaes, 2001; Camp et al, 2003).[1] Private prisons have been included in some recent studies of prison quality, and prison suicide prevention (for example, Liebling 2004). The prison service conducts 'quality of life' prisoner surveys in both public and private sector prisons. The results of these surveys provide comparisons on dimensions such as fairness, safety and staff–prisoner relationships (Standards Audit Unit, 2004). Globally, it is the case that neo-liberal, high-imprisonment, highly punitive, low-equality countries are opting for extensive private sector involvement;

---

[1] The most comprehensive study to date (Rynne, 2005, a PhD on 'The Regime Impacts of Privatization on Prison Quality in Queensland 1989-2000') is facing publication restrictions.

conservative corporatist countries (such as France) are opting for a more limited model (semi-privatisation); and low-imprisonment, social-democratic countries (such as Scandinavia) are so far resisting privatisation entirely (Cavadino and Dignan, 2005).

The evidence to date

The evidence suggests that, at establishment level, high-performing private sector prisons generally do well at providing activity, meeting targets, and treating prisoners respectfully (see, for example, Liebling, 2004; National Audit Office, 2003). Prisoners report better staff–prisoner relationships in many private prisons. There is some evidence that prisoner well-being is higher in high-performing private sector prisons than in public sector prisons and that as a result, suicides may be lower than expected given the populations and turnover (although there are some important exceptions). These tentative findings seem to be related to the lower levels of frustration encountered by prisoners, and the less unionised, less traditional (that is, less cohesive and anti-management) culture deliberately established among staff in the better private prisons. Due to lack of evidence from less well-performing private prisons to date, it is impossible to say whether these findings are due to private sector management, or high performance.

Weaknesses in the private sector tend to be in the area of security, safety, drug control, and the use of authority. This is related to lack of experience and the tendency of prisons in general to find the balancing act between custody and 'care' difficult (for example, see HMCIP, 2003). Standards Audit Unit data suggest that Rye Hill and (to a lesser extent) Parc are doing less well, and are rated very poorly by prisoners on dimensions such as fairness, order and security, and safety.

We should note that these comparisons are only as good as the data on which they are based. There is considerable dispute about how to conceptualise and measure prison quality, as well as difficulties in matching prisons for comparative purposes. There is also disagreement (for example, between Sparks, 1994, and Harding, 1997, 2001) as to whether improvements in prison quality, even where found, justify use of the private sector in the delivery of so-called 'penal services'.

A controversial US study found that 198 releasees from private sector prisons did marginally better on release than a matched sample of 198 releasees from public sector prisons (Lanza-Kaduce et al, 1999). The offences were less serious, and there were slightly fewer of them. This study has been criticised on the grounds that the 12-month follow-up period used was too short, the differences were small, and one of the authors worked for the private company involved (Geis et al, 1999). The explanations offered for the differences found were largely cultural: that is, that private sector staff supported a 'treatment' or programme approach to prison life.

The organisational context supported treatment rather than custody goals. There have been no such follow-up studies conducted in the UK.

Particular and hidden dangers

There is an intriguing paradox at the heart of the privatisation experiment: that the public sector has had difficulty in translating its clearly expressed values into daily practices at ground level, whereas the private sector, at its best, and motivated by expansion and profit, has established reasonably effective ways of ensuring that staff treat prisoners decently, that they deliver regimes, and that they focus on targets. There is a risk that by focusing only on 'on the ground' or 'interior legitimacy' achievements, we forget that the legitimacy deficits may lie further up the chain: in the behaviour of company directors, in exterior places.[2] Lobbying in high places and hard selling of professionally packaged 'services' constitute one set of problematic practices. There are examples of practices in the training of staff, for example, and in the contracts offered for escorts services, where cost savings seem to outweigh other important considerations (the need for experienced staff, and the risks of late receptions into custody).

Lessons identifiable so far

The prison privatisation experiment has resulted in several important lessons:

1. It is important to establish the purpose of competition, and to develop explicit criteria, in order to guide policy making (and so that in-house and external evaluations can address achievements and difficulties against these criteria).
2. The management of public sector prisons required modernising, so that the inculcation of values, and the feeling of accountability, could be better accomplished at ground level.
3. It is true to say that something of a management revolution has occurred in the public sector prison service since 1992, and it is probably the case that the threat of privatisation has contributed to the speed with which this transformation has taken place, and its accomplishment.
4. Private sector prison staff can be managed in ways that ensure more rather than less legitimate treatment of prisoners. This should mean, in principle, that the same is true for public sector staff.
5. There are limits beyond which efficiencies (as well as control by measurement) can become counterproductive, in both sectors.

---

[2] I am drawing here on the language of interior and exterior legitimacy used in Sparks (1994).

6. Start-up phases in the delivery of services by the private sector are always difficult and sometimes dangerous. Security and safety tend to improve with experience.
7. There are major differences between companies – so that (some) values, and performance or quality, may vary more between companies than between the public and the private sector.
8. Performance or quality contests can only be as good as the measures they are based on.
9. Insufficient evaluation of practices, outcomes and broader implications has been carried out. There has to date been no takeover of an existing public sector prison by the private sector.
10. In privately managed prisons, values matter but often for the wrong reasons (they are deontological or moral concepts are being accomplished for instrumental reasons).
11. Instrumentalism, with all its dangers, is increasingly alive and well in the public sector.

Criminal justice practice involves and creates 'special moral environments' (Sparks et al, 1996, p 26). The matter of how people feel treated in criminal justice institutions has serious implications, both for what happens (that is, outcomes), but also, for the claims that can be made about them. The moral values and practices of public and private sector corrections personnel, and the moral climates of their institutions and organisations, should be the subject of careful and reflective scrutiny. We should also bear in mind that prison privatisation may be an alternative policy choice to decarceration.

The applicability of these lessons to the probation service[3]

The problems faced by the probation service are clearly different from those faced by the public sector prison service when privatisation appeared as an attractive solution to escalating costs, overcrowding, and the under-management of culturally resistant prison staff. The management and financial accountability issues may be similar, but some of the cultural problems are almost the reverse. The resistance of probation employees to increased centralisation, as well as to competition, has its roots in a principled objection to the imposition of 'punishment in the community'. What is required under the modernisation agenda for the probation service is increased emphasis on compliance and enforcement, as opposed to the dignifying of staff attitudes sought in the prison service. The ideological 'reshaping' being called for has a very different nature (and therefore has different implications). There are, of course, more mundane concerns with management practices and increased financial accountability (which are easier to justify).

---

[3] I would like to thank Mike Hough for his contribution to this section of the chapter.

The probation service has always been explicitly 'people focused', in contrast to the more mixed value-system at officer level in the prison service. The problem, as I have outlined in more detail elsewhere (Liebling, 2004), is that 'people-focused' values often coincide with 'liberal' values towards punishment, enforcement, and the number of chances offenders should be given when their lives are in chaos. This is a much more contested debate than the one facing prison staff under competition. In the case of the probation service, the underlying assumption from government and senior management is that more control (at the expense of what?) is needed to secure public and judicial confidence. The empirical relationship between 'more control' and successful outcomes, particularly when personal relationships suffer as a result is, however, equivocal (see Hearnden and Millie, 2003; Bottoms et al, 2004). There is also a sense that much had been accomplished since the early 1990s and especially since the establishment of the national probation service in 2000.

Certainly the Home Office saw there to be a problem in the early and mid-1990s with the primacy given to 'care' by probation staff at the expense of 'control', and with the failure of the service to enforce the conditions of probation orders with acceptable rigour. But by 2000 the Home Office had won the battle with the National Association of Police Organisations (Napo) and the probation rank-and-file over these issues pretty decisively. Since then, the rigour of probation enforcement, for example, has continued to improve, and the role of probation in delivering 'punishment in the community' is now an accepted fact of life. In the process, however, the resilience of the workforce appears to have suffered and its morale has fallen. There is a clear risk that in its present state the probation service would be incapacitated rather than energised by the tension that contestability would inject into the system. In contrast to circumstances surrounding the introduction of prison privatisation, there is now a persuasive argument that a period of stability in probation with strong, supportive, consistent management, would do more to rebuild probation morale and sense of purpose than further upheaval. In other words, the National Offender Management Service (NOMS) would be wise to move only slowly towards contestability, and to expose only a limited range of services to 'contestation'. It remains to be seen whether such cautious incrementalism is politically acceptable.

There are unresolved issues for both the prison service and the probation service concerning how poor-performing providers are dealt with (or more likely, coped with), when the demands of high case loads, overloaded courts, and overcrowded prisons are the substance of everyday life.

It is more likely that the voluntary sector will have a role to play in probation contestability – so that a three-way competition (with new partnerships emerging) is more likely to evolve than the two-way competition that so far characterises competition to run prisons. Again, this is likely to pose certain threats to voluntary sector values (such as protecting the interests of disadvantaged groups and limiting the role of coercive strategies in crime control; see CLINKS, 2005). This may be an opportune moment to explore the role and significance of 'commitment to public service' in successful work with offenders. Certainly it is clear that in some fields the private sector can combine profit with both technical excellence and commitment to the well-being of their 'customers'. Private health care providers provide the obvious example. However, there are good reasons for thinking that organisations that aim to persuade offenders to improve their standards of behaviour are best staffed by altruistically motivated workers, and that the public and voluntary sectors may be better able to recruit and retain people with these qualities than the private sector.

For the present, however, there is no evidence either to support or refute the idea that altruistically motivated staff will outperform more instrumentally orientated staff in working with offenders. There is little sign either in the Carter report (Carter, 2003) or the Home Office response to it (NOMS, 2005) that this issue has been given any serious consideration. Decisions of such importance in the evolution of criminal justice practices and values should not be taken in an evidential vacuum. A detailed programme of research and evaluation, which includes these questions of motivation and the organisation of working practices, should be carried out.

Conclusion

Prior to 1991, there were self-evident problems in the occupational as well as management culture of the prisons workforce that needed correcting. These problems included indifferent or oppressive attitudes towards prisoners in many establishments, and a lack of responsiveness to management and government requirements. While there is still dispute as to whether privatisation was the only way to address these difficulties, and they have only been overcome to some extent, it is difficult to defend the pre-1991 state of play on moral grounds. With the probation service, matters are not so straightforward. It is unclear whether 'people changing practice' can be made more effective through the discipline of the marketplace:

> My own prejudice is that the key question for probation practice is not 'what works', but 'who works?' The social and personal skills needed to persuade people to change their behaviour may not be readily engineered through conventional private sector management processes. We really need to know whether or not this is the case before we make any wholesale commitment to contestability in NOMS. (Hough, personal communication, 2005)

There will continue to be problems in conceptualising and developing appropriate targets in the awarding of contracts (as well as in interpreting the scores). We should be watching carefully to track whether the presence of commercial interests in prison and probation work has a distorting effect on national and regional policy. As other countries rapidly turn to the UK to see what our experience to date has taught us, and as they bow to the same (or even greater) pressure to privatise, we should be armed with rigorous evidence, and a much fuller account of the lessons learned. There can be benefits from contestability in the right circumstances, but there are also risks and there may be some unintended consequences. The debate needs to move from its basis in faith, or stringent opposition, to evidence.

References
Bottomley, A.K., James, A., Clare, E. and Liebling, A. (1997) *Monitoring and Evaluation of Wolds Remand Prison*, Home Office Report, London: Home Office.

Bottoms, A.E, Rex, S. and Robinson, G. (2004) *Alternatives to Prison: Options for an Insecure Society*, Cullompton: Willan Publishing.

Camp, S.G. and Gaes, G.G. (2001) 'Private adult prisons: what do we really know and why don't we know more?', in D. Shichor and M.J. Gilbert (eds) *Privatisation in Criminal Justice: Past, Present and Future*, Ohio, OH: Anderson Publishing, pp 283-98.

Camp, S.G., Gaes, G.G., Klein-Saffran, J., Daggett, D.M. and Saylor, W. (2003) 'Using inmate survey data in assessing prison performance: a case study comparing private and public prisons', *Criminal Justice Review*, vol 27, no 1, pp 26-51.

Carter, P. (2003) *Managing Offenders, Reducing Crime: A New Approach*, London: Prime Minister's Strategy Unit.

Cavadino, P. and Dignan, P. (2005) *Penal Systems: A Comparative Approach*, London: Sage Publications.

CLINKS (2005) NOMS Conference 7 July, Summary of key points (written by A. Liebling) available at www.clinks.org

Geis, G., Mobley, A. and Schicor, D. (1999) 'Private Prisons, Criminological Research and Conflict of Interest: A Case Study', *Crime and Delinquency*, vol 45, no 3, pp 372-88.

Harding, R. (1997) *Private Prisons and Public Accountability*, New Brunswick, NJ: Transaction Publishers.

Harding, R. (2001) 'Private prisons', in M. Tonry and J. Petersilia (eds) *Crime and Justice: A Review of Research*, Chicago, IL: University of Chicago Press, pp 265-346.

Hearnden, I. and Millie, A. (2003) *Investigating Links Between Probation Enforcement and Reconviction*, Home Office Online report 41/03, London: Home Office.

HMCIP (HM Chief Inspector of Prisons) (2003) Report on a Full Announced Inspection of HMP and YOI Ashfield 1-5 July 2002 by HM Chief Inspector of Prisons, London: Home Office.

Home Office (1988) *Private Sector Involvement in the Remand System*, Cm. 434, London: HMSO.

Home Office (2000) *Modernising the Management of the Prison Service: An Independent Report by the Targeted Performance Initiative Working Group – The Laming Report*, London: Home Office.

House of Commons (1987) Fourth Report from the Home Affairs Committee, Session 1986-87: Contract Provision of Prisons (HC 291), London: HMSO.

James, A.K., Bottomley, A.K., Liebling, A. and Clare, E. (1997) *Privatizing Prisons: Rhetoric and Reality*, London: Sage Publications.

King, R.D. and McDermott, K. (1989) 'British prisons 1970-1987: the ever-deepening crisis', *British Journal of Criminology*, vol 29, pp 107-28.

Lanza-Kaduce, L., Parker, K.F. and Thomas, C.W. (1999) 'A comparative recidivism analysis of releasees from private and public prisons', *Crime and Delinquency*, vol 45, no 1, pp 28-47.

Liebling, A. (2004) *Prisons and their Moral Performance: A Study of Values, Quality and Prison Life*, Oxford: Clarendon Press.

Moyle, P (1995) 'Private prison research in Queensland, Australia: a case study of Borrallon Correctional Centre, 1991', *British Journal of Criminology*, vol 31, no 1, pp 34-62.

Moyle, P. (2001) 'Separating the allocation of punishment from its administration: theoretical and empirical observations', *British Journal of Criminology*, vol 41, no 1, pp 77-100.

National Audit Office (2003) The Operational Performance of PFI Prisons Report by the Comptroller and Auditor General HC Session 2002-2003: 18 June 2003, London: The Stationery Office.

NOMS (National Offender Management Service) (2005) *Together We Can Reduce Re-offending and Increase Public Confidence*, London: NOMS.

Park, I. (2000) *Review of Comparative Costs and Performance of Privately and Publicly Operated Prisons 1998-1999*, Home Office Statistical Bulletin 6/00, London: Home Office.

Sparks, R. (1994) 'Can prisons be legitimate? Penal politics, privatisation and the timeliness of an old idea', in special issue of *British Journal of Criminology* (1994) published separately by Oxford University Press as R. King and M. Maguire (eds) *Prisons in Context*.

Sparks, R., Bottoms, A.E. and Hay, W. (1996) *Prisons and the Problem of Order*, Oxford: Clarendon Press.

Standards Audit Unit (2004) 'MQPL [Measuring the Quality of Prison Life] Survey Research Reports', internal publications made available to author, Corby: HM Prison Service.

Woodbridge, J. (1999) *A Comparison of the Costs of Public and Privately Managed Prisons*, London: HMSO.

7

A modern service, fit for purpose?

David Faulkner

NOMS – its origin and purpose

Most of the reactions to the creation of the National Offender Management Service (NOMS), and to the original Carter report (Carter, 2003) and the government's response (Home Office, 2004) on which it was based, have been critical, or at best sceptical. Critics have focused mainly on the break-up, or some of them would say destruction, of the probation service (Nellis, 2004); the implications of 'contestability'; the early lack of consultation; and the absence, as they saw it, of a clear justification or rationale. More general criticisms have been that the real aim of the reform is a political and ideological attempt to create a 'market' in penal treatment, with as much of the penal system as possible transferred to the private sector; that the reform is part of a wider policy of expanding the 'net' of punishment and criminal justice in the interests of social cohesion and control; and that a set of impersonal, mechanistic interventions will displace human and personal relationships with offenders.[1] Others have variously welcomed the reform as providing a necessary division between purchasing and providing, and between policy and operations; a basis for achieving a balance between capacity and demand (or more optimistically a reduction in the use of imprisonment); a more coherent and socially responsible approach to the resettlement of offenders; and perhaps the foundation for a service that has a stronger sense of identity, purpose and pride. This chapter tries to show how that more optimistic vision might be realised.

Three fundamental questions are: What is the purpose of the new service?; How should it achieve that purpose?; and What kind of service ought it to be? The first can be endlessly debated, as similar questions about prisons and probation have been debated in the past, but the government hopes to have settled it in the five purposes which it has set out in the Corporate Plan (Home Office 2005a). They are the protection of the public; the reduction of re-offending; the proper

---

[1] See, for example, Davies, N. (2005) 'A system in chaos', *The Guardian*, 23 June.

punishment of offenders; ensuring offenders' awareness of the effects of crime on victims and the public; and the rehabilitation of offenders. Arguments will inevitably continue over the different purposes' relationship with one another, the potential conflict between them, the priority to be given to each of them in particular cases or sets of circumstances, and over the government's perceptions of punishment more generally, especially the change of emphasis from 'desert' to public protection (McConville, 2003; Zedner, 2004; also the articles on punishment and rehabilitation in Criminal Justice Matters, no 60, Summer, 2005).

The methods for achieving those purposes are set out in the Corporate Plan – to implement the orders of the courts and supervise offenders and those remanded in custody in such a way as to protect the public; to provide a range of effective interventions and services that are designed to reduce re-offending; to give offenders the opportunity to lead law-abiding, productive and healthy lives; and to work in a way that treats offenders fairly and with decency. Issues will continue to arise over the type of 'interventions' and 'opportunities' that are suitable or 'effective' in different cases or circumstances, and about how the concepts of fairness and decency are to be understood and applied in practice.

The success of NOMS will depend on how those continuing arguments and issues come to be resolved, and so on the answer to the third question – what kind of service ought it to be? That depends in turn on its culture and values and how those are sustained by its arrangements for governance and accountability. There has been little or no public discussion of those arrangements so far.

A comparison with economics

In a different area of policy, and coming from a different academic discipline, the American economist and Nobel Prize winner Douglass North (1997) has examined the process of economic change and the failure of economics to solve the problems of development. In a recent (May 2005) lecture in Oxford, he restated his argument that conventional approaches are narrow and static, when they should be broad and dynamic; and that in a rapidly changing world there are no 'basics' to which it is possible to return for a fresh start. Progress has to be by a process of evolution, drawn from a country's own cultural heritage, using local and informal structures, proceeding by trial and error, and avoiding rigid or elaborate rules. There should be more emphasis on rewards for success than on punishment for failure, on initiative than on conformity, and on negotiation and consent than on direction and command.

The analogy between economic development and tackling crime should not be pressed too far. But North's analysis may suggest a similar approach to the difficulty that governments have always found in solving the problems of crime by reforming the criminal justice process or the penal system. His vision of a modern economy could inform a parallel vision of a modern approach to crime and social disorder, and an understanding of the part that criminal justice – and especially NOMS – could have in that vision. NOMS would then be more a federation of locally managed and locally accountable services and partnerships than a monolithic, impersonal, top-down organisation, managed in detail from the centre. It would have an important place for 'contestability', but as a means of introducing diversity, innovation and experiment, not to promote competition for its own sake or simply to drive down costs. The culture would be one of challenge, achievement and reward, and of mutual respect and responsibility in which those qualities are shown to offenders as well as expected from them.[2] It should not be one of conformity, blame and aversion to risk. It should not see offenders and others who do not 'fit' as different, separate and dangerous; deny them dignity and respect; or treat them as a problem to be managed or an enemy to be defeated. NOMS will need to take full advantage of new technology, both for information and communication and for the supervision and control of offenders (both electronic monitoring and satellite tracking), but it should do so with humanity and respect (Nellis, 2004, 2005). Development and adjustment would be a continuous process.

The service would not be built to a model of centralised command, as the prison service has been in the past and still is today, nor would it be constructed from a series of centrally or regionally negotiated commercial or quasi-commercial contracts. Within a national framework of legislation, standards and financial controls, the service's governance and 'ownership' would be shared between central government and local communities, users and stakeholders. Ministers and Parliament would hold it to account for its financial performance and its compliance with legislation and government policy; communities, users and stakeholders would do so for its effect on communities, its contribution to their well-being (including but not confined to the protection of the public), and its treatment of individuals. Staff should think of themselves as members of a single profession, with a sense of pride in themselves and trust in their colleagues and confidence that they are valued and will be fairly treated by their employers and by government. That will be difficult if not impossible in a situation of commercial competition and

---

[2] That culture is arguably part of the British, or English, tradition and national identity. A lot has been written about national identity, usually from a perspective that wants to promote a more unified version and often in a spirit of nostalgia for what is thought to have been a more orderly and cohesive society at some time in the past. The hope in this chapter is that the tradition of liberal humanity that has been present, although not always dominant, in English penal practice will survive and recover its influence, both in politics and in NOMS; that it will meet the challenges from those forces which oppose it; and that it will continue to inspire those who work with offenders in whatever capacity. Tonry (2004) has argued that what he sees as the prevailing spirit of punitivism is one of the peculiarities of the English character. Mike Nellis (2004) hopes that, so far as it exists, it is more a temporary result of the present configuration of English politics.

confidentially,[3] and NOMS itself, in the NOMS Update,[4] recognises the danger of 'unhelpfully adversarial relationships'.

A service constructed on those lines would more closely fit the description of what the government might call a 'modern service, fit for purpose', and involve fewer political risks to itself than one which was under tight central control. It is hard to tell how far it might correspond with the model that Carter had in mind. Neither the Carter report nor the government's response contains any 'story' or 'narrative' that could give a sense of conviction to the proposals, and any larger vision that could inspire the new service will have to come from elsewhere. In former times, that vision could have been publicly expressed in the report of a departmental committee or Royal Commission, or in a White Paper. It must now be created internally. The NOMS Update states that 'It will be very important to create a shared vision of the future NOMS world that everyone will support enthusiastically. We are working to make this happen by developing an overall NOMS Operating Model in collaboration with key stakeholders'.

Criteria for success

Successive governments and their critics have for several years sought to gain political advantage by portraying the criminal justice system as 'failing' (Home Office, 1997, 2003; Blair, 2004; Howard, 2005). They have been helped by the public's widespread ignorance of the subject and ambivalence towards it (Roberts and Hough, 2002, 2005), and by the complexity of the statistics and the inconclusive results of much of the research. So long as crime and criminal justice remain political issues, it will be difficult to base a convincing claim to success on statistics or surveys, the results of which are always likely to be contested politically and in the media.[5]

The government has set a reduction in rates of reconviction and an increase in public confidence as tests by which the success of the new Service will be judged. The first depends on the cooperation of other agencies and of the public in the resettlement of offenders, and on the wider social and economic factors which affect levels of crime more generally. The second will be influenced by the public's understanding of the facts and by its degree of confidence in government and public institutions as a whole. Neither can be aimed at directly nor achieved by the

---

[3] HM Chief Inspector of Prisons noted in her inspection report on HM Prison Wolds that the growing distance between private and public sector prisons was a distinct disadvantage in sentence planning and resettlement – what is now to be called 'offender management' and one of the main public justifications for the reform. See www.homeoffice.gov.uk/docs4/Final_draft_Wolds.pdf

[4] Issue 5, 2005, available at: www.noms.homeoffice.gov.uk/news-publications

[5] Government must also beware of overstating positive results (Bottoms, 2005).

Service on its own. They are situations to be achieved and sustained, not targets to be hit. Failure to achieve them could not be attributed simply to the Service's own performance, and would be a matter for which the government, or society, as a whole should take responsibility.

NOMS is more likely to be judged in practice on the extent to which the service "works" – whether what is supposed to happen does happen, at the right time, in the right place and for the right people, and whether offenders complete programmes and comply with orders and conditions. Courts, other services and voluntary organisations must be able to rely on NOMS to work with them in a spirit of genuine cooperation and understanding, and on equal and mutually agreed terms. Staff, offenders, their families and victims need to know that they will be properly treated, where they stand and what they can expect. Those things do not always happen at present, for various reasons which include pressures on resources and prison overcrowding, but sometimes also the effect of nationally imposed targets and league tables.[6]

NOMS must be efficient and effective, but it must also have authority and legitimacy. It must earn the trust and respect of its own staff, of other services and individuals with whom it is in direct contact, and of the general public. Management and staff must be listened to, believed and taken seriously. Like all public services, NOMS must be fair, transparent and accountable in all its dealings and contacts. Its accountability must run not only upwards to ministers and Parliament, but also in other directions and through a variety of mechanisms to the organisations, communities and individuals who are affected by its work (for a fuller discussion, see Faulkner, 2005). Systematic ethnic monitoring and relations with minority ethnic communities and their leaders and representatives are an important aspect. Effective accountability is especially important for a service that exercises coercive powers on behalf of the state, including enforcement of the ultimate power of loss of liberty. It must exercise those powers and functions legitimately, proportionately, and so far as possible with the consent of those who are affected by them (Sparks et al, 1996; see also Alison Liebling's chapter in this volume, Chapter 6).

As Carter recognised, a necessary condition for success is a stable balance between the capacity of the service and the demands that are made upon it. That is partly a matter for the service's relationship with the courts (see below), but planning for that capacity is especially difficult at a time when crime is falling but the government is constantly expanding the scope reach of the criminal justice process and with it the penal system as part of its wider policies for public protection and social control.

---

[6] See the vivid, if contentious, account in Nick Davies' articles in *The Guardian,* 22 and 23 June, 2005. For a discussion of the effect of targets on policing, see Neyroud and Beckley (2001).

Relationship with ministers: policy and operations

The relationship between the prison service and ministers or the central Home Office has never been easy or straightforward. Ministers or the central Home Office have at various times sought greater administrative integration (the dissolution of the Prison Commission in 1963), or political control (during the mid-1990s – Dunbar and Langdon, 1998). The prison service itself has always sought greater operational independence and respect for its professional experience and judgement, often with a (sometimes misplaced) insistence on the 'unity' of the service. Greater independence was theoretically achieved when the service became an executive agency in the early 1990s, although the change was driven more by the Treasury as a means of achieving greater efficiency and accountability than by any respect for the service itself. The independence and supposed ineffectiveness of local probation services were a source of frustration for ministers during the 1990s, leading first to the establishment of National Standards and then to the creation of the national probation service and the National Probation Directorate in 2001.

The distinction between 'policy' and 'operations' has at different times been denied (when the prison service first became an agency), and thereafter asserted (later in the 1990s, to hold managers more effectively to account – or sometimes, it might be said, to enable ministers to escape any responsibility of their own). Ministers have increasingly imposed their own political judgement on the professional judgement of officials and practitioners, and on the findings of research.

The lesson from that experience is that there is an important distinction to be observed between three types of consideration – the interests of services themselves; the wider public or national interest; and the electoral advantage of the government of the day. In broad terms, they are respectively considerations of 'operations', policy', and 'politics'. The first is essentially a matter for the services themselves; the second is or was at one time considered to be the province of administrative civil servants and of ministers in their capacity as servants of the Crown; the third is for ministers and their political advisers. The boundaries cannot be clearly defined in day-to-day practice and in recent years they have often been deliberately obscured. Some judgements can be made on the basis of one of those considerations without much regard to the other two; some will involve all three. There may be a conflict between them. In those situations it is essential for the integrity of government administration that all the considerations are properly identified and taken into account in the decision-making process, and that the process itself is open and accountable.

In NOMS, 'public interest' or 'policy' considerations will be an important part of the 'commissioning' role held by the national and regional offender managers. Their judgements should be clearly distinguishable from 'operational' judgements made in the interests of services or service providers, whether in the public, private or voluntary sector. It needs to be recognised and respected in working relationships, and so far as possible in organisational structures.

One requirement for NOMS will be a strong and coherent policy group that will, with ministers, set the direction of penal policy; negotiate with the Treasury the share of national resources that should be devoted to the penal system; determine the size and shape of its custodial, non-custodial and intermediate components; and make judgements about the nature, effectiveness and propriety of different forms of penal treatment and experience. The group will need to engage effectively not only with ministers but also with other parts of Whitehall and Westminster. That function is fragmented at present. How it should relate to commissioning, and whether it should be located within NOMS, the wider Home Office, or a separate Department of Justice, are serious questions for the longer term, especially if the need to prevent and suppress terrorism results in a Home Office that becomes essentially a department of home security. More immediate, but very significant, questions will concern the role of the Permanent Secretary and Chief Executive as Accounting Officers, and the position of the Audit Commission and the National Audit Office in relation to the new service.

However those questions are resolved, the service will need relationships between ministers, administrative officials and operational staff that are based on mutual trust, understanding and respect for each other's experience, authority and judgement. Ministers must allow space for professional leadership that is independent of their own political interest, and professional leaders must resist any temptation to become political figures themselves.

Relationships within NOMS

Relationships within NOMS itself will also be crucial – between the 'commissioning' and 'providing' arms, and between the centre, regions and local areas. There are inevitably entrenched interests to be protected and territory to be fought for. Clarity, agreement and acceptance will be needed about who is responsible for what, who has authority over whom, the nature of that authority, and the spirit in which it is to be exercised.

The commissioning arm should now be responsible for 'policy', with a clearer division between 'policy' and 'operations' than has existed for some time. The prison service seems secure in its 'providing' or 'operational' function and its present structure, but the future of the probation service is less certain. Many of its staff will probably become offender managers, but it is not yet clear in what kind of structure or organisation; others will be 'providers' in what might be a new national service, or an amorphous and 'contestable' set of 'public service interventions'. Probation boards may continue for the time being, but their longer-term future is uncertain.

Critical questions include the functions and accountability of regional offender managers; the functions, accountability and status of offender managers; the relationship between them; and the relationship between both and the prison service, 'public service interventions' and contractors or partners in the private and voluntary and community sectors. In an earlier NOMS Update, for June 2005,[7] Martin Narey stated that 'through the transfer of service specification and purchase from the existing provider [regional offender managers are to start] commissioning all prison and probation services as early as April 2006'. The objective is to be to 'raise performance levels', and the only reference to 'policy' is to 'Ministerial policy on contestability'. At this stage, the change seems to involve the creation of an alternative or additional bureaucratic process, but no suggestion of any transformation or revitalisation of penal practice, or indication of how such a transformation might be inspired or informed. Commissioning seems at present to be seen as a high-level process, regionalised for administrative convenience but with no indication of any regional identity or accountability and some distance removed from the task of constructing local situations, schemes or relationships that would benefit individual offenders, victims or communities and achieve some reconciliation between them. That task is being carried forward separately, often under difficult conditions. It is especially important in relation to minority ethnic communities, and to disaffected young people within those communities and in the country as a whole.

Offender management is arguably the most important justification for the reform, and one of the service's main strands of work. The NOMS Delivery Team has designed an Offender Management Model, which is to be implemented and delivered across England and Wales. But it is not yet clear how offender managers will be organised or enabled to do the work; what authority they will have to give directions to service providers or to commission facilities; what cooperation they can expect from agencies or communities outside the criminal justice system; whether the distribution of the prison population and the demands on themselves will enable them to have any continuing or consistent relationship with offenders or their families; and if not, how that crucial and recently neglected relationship can be provided (see Peter Raynor's and Mike Maguire's chapter in this volume – Chapter 3; also McNeill et al, 2005; and Robinson, 2005). Further questions include the arrangements for their line management and their employment status (whether they will be employed by the government itself or by probation boards, or whether they will or could properly be employed by private sector contractors); and their standing in local communities, the courts, and among colleagues in other criminal justice services. Offender managers probably ought to be the service's representatives on bodies such as local criminal justice boards and crime and disorder reduction partnerships, but they will need the seniority, credibility and time to do so effectively.

---

[7] Also available at: www.noms.homeoffice.gov.uk/news-publications

Courts

As already stated, a necessary condition for NOMS to succeed is a stable balance between the demands on the service and its capacity to meet those demands – in the fullest sense of accommodation, facilities, what are now called 'interventions', techniques and skills. Prison overcrowding is only one of the pressures on prison and probation resources, and the need to match capacity to the number and type of sentences imposed by the court, or vice versa, has been an issue for the last 40 years. The Carter report has for the first time made a clear official statement of the need for a closer alignment between sentencing practice and the capacity of the system, with reductions both in the level of the prison population and in the number of offenders under supervision from those that were then projected. Projections for the prison population at that time (December 2003) ranged from 76,000 to 87,500 in mid-2011, depending on the scenarios chosen. Those figures have now been increased to 76,520 and 90,780 respectively, and the actual population was 76,506 on 22 July 2005. Carol Hedderman's chapter in this volume (Chapter 4) discusses whether the NOMS strategy will succeed in containing that growth.

The 2003 Criminal Justice Act will demand a new relationship between the NOMS and the courts. The main instrument for that purpose is the Sentencing Guidelines Council, set up under the 2003 Criminal Justice Act, supported by the Sentencing Advisory Panel originally established under the 1998 Crime and Disorder Act and with a statutory duty to take account of the cost and effectiveness of sentences (under Section 170 of the 2003 Criminal Justice Act), and the availability of resources (if the Management of Offenders and Sentencing Bill is enacted in the form in which it was introduced in the previous Parliament). The balance cannot, however, be achieved without the cooperation of the courts on a local and day-to-day basis. The process of assembling and disseminating that information, and the use that the Council and the courts make of it, will be matters of considerable delicacy.

For courts themselves, the statutory purposes of sentencing introduced by Section 142 of the 2003 Act (punishment, reduction of crime, reform and rehabilitation of offenders, protection of the public and reparation) correspond roughly with those for NOMS itself. They ought to require sentencers to take account not only of the sentencing guidelines, but also to consider and state the purposes to be achieved by particular sentences for particular offenders. NOMS, probably working through offender managers, should help the court to decide what those purposes might be, what services or facilities are needed to achieve them, and then make sure that those services or facilities are actually provided. That will be a new situation, but similar procedures are already being followed for drug treatment and testing orders and for some priority and prolific offenders. The NOMS Update for August 2005 states that 'we have worked to secure the agreement of the senior judiciary to the establishment of local sentencer/NOMS communications fora', and that new forms for court reports are being developed to advise sentencers on available options.

It will be interesting to see whether the Crown Prosecution Service comes to play a part in the process. The Lord Chief Justice, Lord Woolf, discussed some of the issues in his Leon Radzinowicz memorial lecture (Woolf, 2005): the tentative way in which he did so shows the sensitivity of the subject.

Local services, authorities and communities

Local involvement with the public and local responsiveness have now become prominent themes in other public services, including the police, but it is not clear how far there will be any similar emphasis in NOMS.

It is universally acknowledged that the successful resettlement of offenders, and therefore any prospect of reducing rates of re-offending, depend on the cooperation of local services, authorities and communities, including minority communities (SEU, 2002; House of Common Select Committee on Home Affairs, 2004). Their cooperation depends in turn on mutual understanding, trust and goodwill, both in bi-lateral relationships and in groups such as local criminal justice boards and crime and disorder reduction partnerships. But the prison service has no tradition of engaging either courts or local communities in the management of its own institutions, and the tradition of local involvement that previously existed in the probation service has been largely extinguished by earlier reforms. NOMS must be able to engage with the relevant organisations, groups and individuals in ways that are both proactive and responsive. Offender managers are likely to be the most important points of contact, which will often be at a very local level. NOMS will need to organise itself and deploy its resources so that its members have the authority, local standing, skills and, very importantly, time to be effective in those relationships. Local authorities have a significant and so far largely unrecognised contribution to make (LGA, 2005). The Office of the Deputy Prime Minister (ODPM, 2005) has published separate papers on 'citizen engagement' with local services, making important points about local leadership and representation and the empowerment of local neighbourhoods. The subject is now being widely discussed in lectures and seminars, by ministers among others, but mainly in the context of local government and without reference to NOMS or criminal justice.

NOMS and civil renewal

The government published Together We Can, its Action Plan for Civil Renewal, in June 2005 (Home Office, 2005b). The Action Plan contains a significant section headed 'Together we can reduce re-offending and raise public confidence in the criminal justice system'. The intended outcome is that 'communities have more understanding and influence over the activities of the Criminal Justice System [CJS] and are able to work with CJS agencies in reducing re-offending' (pp 17-19) . Action is to include support for local criminal justice boards in their work to engage and involve local people; developing the pilot Community Justice Centre in Liverpool and the Salford Community Justice Initiative; effective use of community engagement in establishing and implementing offender management policies and practices; and opportunities for work by offenders to meet local concerns, improve the local environment, and be made more visible.

The scope for NOMS to contribute to civil renewal, and the potential significance of its contribution, has been discussed elsewhere (Faulkner and Flaxington, 2004). The Home Office has published and sought comments on a draft strategy (Home Office, 2005c), and the outcome is to be published later in the year.

The connection between civil renewal and the work of NOMS – and of other parts of the criminal justice system – is important. The optimistic view is that civil renewal will reassert a set of liberal and inclusive values, and with it a part of the British tradition and culture that is in danger of being overwhelmed by the forces of globalisation and managerialism, and by a politics and a set of public attitudes that appeals to individualism and narrow self-interest. Those values matter not only politically but also because they then shape the professional culture of NOMS and other criminal justice services, the reasons for which people choose to work for them, the reactions of those who become involved with them, and the confidence and trust that they receive from the public.

There may be a danger that civil renewal will become a programme (or as David Blunkett called it an 'ethos') that is based not so much on liberal, open and democratic values as one designed to increase the power and influence of government; to conscript citizens, communities and voluntary organisations to serve its own political purposes; and to subject them to its own mechanisms of control – public service agreements, service level agreements, targets, performance measures and the rest. A report prepared for the National Council for Voluntary Organisations (Jochum et al, 2005) suggests that the government's interest in civil renewal is primarily to further its own agendas, and that voluntary and community organisations and wider civil society are likely to have different perceptions. There may be a further danger that if policies for criminal justice and civil renewal are brought too close together, they will become combined as a means of imposing social control through an ever-expanding process of criminalisation and punishment.

Three further points arise. First, citizens and communities including minority communities will need the capacity to respond to the opportunities that civil renewal and NOMS provide, and the power and responsibility to do so constructively and in a spirit of public duty and service. Building local capacity – and with it responsibility – may be as important for the 'commissioners' in NOMS as the provision of actual services or interventions.

Second, civil renewal and active citizenship should not be seen as a matter that is only for people outside the system. It should also be a matter for staff. They should be enabled and encouraged to play their own part as members of their own communities, both as informal 'ambassadors' for the service and in interpreting their communities' views and feelings back to the service. Contacts such as those might be one of the most effective means of explaining what NOMS is and what it does, of enabling views and feelings to be heard and understood, and so of increasing public confidence.

Third, offenders, including prisoners, should themselves have the opportunity to be active citizens and responsible human beings, within their limits of their situation. Work for the benefit of local communities is an obvious example, but there are many other possibilities including those that have been discussed elsewhere under such headings of the 'Responsible Prisoner' and 'Prisoners as Citizens' (Pryor, 2001; Farrant and Levenson, 2002; Faulkner, 2002).

Research

Research on crime and criminal justice raises important questions about capacity, quality, methodology, the relationship between research institutions and government, commissioning and funding (Hood, 2002). Those questions are beyond the scope of this chapter. But there are two points to be made. The question for NOMS should not be 'What research do we need?' but 'What information and understanding does NOMS need to do its job, and how can that best be provided – research, monitoring, consultation, dialogue, debate?' What can be learned from existing material, and what needs new research and of what kind? What procedures and mechanisms are available, or need to be established? Who has what to contribute? In the new context of NOMS, those questions include but go well beyond the 'effectiveness' of 'programmes' or 'interventions'. They include the dynamics of the various relationships, not only within NOMS and with the offenders with whom it has to deal, but also with the wider world of communities, courts, services and organisations with which NOMS now has to engage.

Second, there has been little recognition that research and statistics are an important mechanism of public accountability, to be used not just for the benefit of government and its agencies but in the service of the country as a whole. The value of information and the cost of obtaining it should be judged not just by its usefulness to managers or politically to ministers, but as part of the service's accountability to Parliament, its stakeholders and the public. Research should be commissioned and carried out independently of NOMS and not limited to the purposes of NOMS as management sees them. NOMS should not see research as another service that can be commissioned or purchased like any other. Some of the most important research is funded by independent institutions, but inevitably on a limited scale. Government must continue to support criminal justice research, but as in other areas of public policy the commissioning authority should be independent of NOMS and of ministers, and should be either a separate research council or the existing Economic and Social Research Council with a ring-fenced budget.

Conclusion

A society's penal system is a reflection of itself. It belongs to society as a whole. Governments on behalf of society must sustain the system and introduce reforms when they are needed. But governments should not treat it as their own exclusive property, or use it as an instrument with which to achieve their own political objectives. Its ownership should be shared with citizens more generally, with those who work in it, with its stakeholders, and in some respects with those whom it detains or supervises. That ownership carries responsibilities, which government and managers should allow, encourage and sometimes require citizens to discharge. They should not effectively remove those responsibilities, either by ignoring them or by prescribing them in too much detail.

Specifically and more immediately, NOMS now needs to:

- establish a strong professional identity, based on a shared vision and clearly articulated inclusive values; and a strong local presence – with courts, other services and organisations and communities – based on mutual confidence and respect including respect for offenders, victims and their families;
- develop the structures, expertise, relationships and mechanisms of accountability to support that identity and presence, with implications for probation boards, independent monitoring boards and local criminal justice boards among others;
- work towards a comprehensive strategy for recruitment, training and career development, for its future leaders and for the service as a whole;
- help other organisations and communities, including minority communities, to develop their own capacity to respond and contribute, with a sense of shared ownership of the issues and solutions;
- use 'contestability' creatively and flexibly for those purposes, in a spirit of equal partnership rather than commercial competition;
- achieve national and local understandings with the courts about the capacity that is available, and about what sentences can realistically be expected to achieve both generally and in particular cases.

There is a point where too liberal an approach to offending and penal treatment would clearly be unacceptable, and another where too repressive an approach could be equally repugnant. They are hard to define and they are a long way apart. They can be moved, to some extent, by information and explanation. Between them there is scope for innovation, initiative and imagination. The challenge for NOMS is to exploit that scope to the full, within the proper limits of accountability and safety and on a basis of sound professional judgement and leadership. The challenge for ministers is to allow NOMS the space to do so.

References

Blair, T. (2004) 'A New Consensus on Law and Order', available at: www.number-10.gov.uk/output/Page6129.asp

Bottoms, A. (2005) 'Methodology matters', *Safer Society*, no 10, pp 10-12.

Carter, P. (2003) *Managing Offenders, Reducing Crime: A New Approach*, London: Prime Minister's Strategy Unit.

Dunbar, I. and Langdon, A. (1998) *Tough Justice: Sentencing and Plural Policies in the 1990s*, London: Blackstone.

Farrant, F. and Levenson, J. (2002) *Barred Citizens*, London: Prison Reform Trust.

Faulkner, D. (2002) 'Prisoners as citizens', *Prison Service Journal*, no 143, pp 46-7.

Faulkner, D. (2005) 'Relationships, accountability and responsibility in the National Offender Management Service', *Public Money and Management*, vol 25, no 5, pp 299-306.

Faulkner, D. and Flaxington, F. (2004) 'NOMS and Civil Renewal', *Vista*, vol 9, no 2, pp 90-9.

Home Office (1997) *No More Excuses*, London: Home Office.

Home Office (2003) *Justice for All*, Cm 5563, London: Home Office.

Home Office (2004) *Reducing Crime, Changing Lives*, London: Home Office.

Home Office (2005a) *National Offender Management Service, Corporate Plan 2005-06 to 2007-08*, London: Home Office.

Home Office (2005b) *Together We Can: The Government Action Plan for Civil Renewal*, London: Home Office.

Home Office (2005c) 'Together we can reduce re-offending and increase public confidence', available at: www.homeoffice.gov.uk/docs4/Final_NOMS_Draft_strategy.pdf

Hood, R. (2002) 'Criminal and penal policy: the vital role of empirical research', in A. Bottoms and M. Tonry (eds) *Ideology, Crime and Criminal Justice*, Cullompton: Willan Publishing.

House of Commons Select Committee on Home Affairs (2004) 'Report of an inquiry into the rehabilitation of offenders, first report session 2004-2005', available at: www.publications.parliament.uk/pa/cm200405/cmselect.cmhaff/193/19303.htm

Howard, M. (2005) 'I believe the punishment should fit the crime', advertisement in *The Sunday Times*, 6 February.

Jochum, V., Pratten, B. and Wilding, K. (2005) *Civil Renewal and Active Citizenship: A Guide to the Debate*, London: National Council for Voluntary Organisations.

LGA (Local Government Association) (2005) 'Going straight: reducing re-offending in local communities', available at: www.lga.gov.uk

McConville, S. (ed) (2003) *The Use of Punishment*, Cullompton: Willan Publishing.

McNeill, F., Batchelor, S., Burnett, R. and Knox, J. (2005) *21st Century Social Work: Reducing Re-offending: Key Practice Skills*, Edinburgh: Scottish Executive.

Nellis, M. (2004) '"Into the field of corrections": the end of English probation in the early 21st century', *Cambrian Law Review*, no 35, pp 115-33.

Nellis, M. (2005) 'Out of this world: the advent of the satellite tracking of offenders in England and Wales', *Howard Journal*, vol 44, no 2, pp 125-50.

Neyroud, P. and Beckley, A. (2001) *Policing Ethics and Human Rights*, Cullompton: Willan Publishing.

North, D. (1997) The Process of Economic Change, Research Paper No. 18, Helsinki: World Institute for Development Economic Research.

ODPM (Office of the Deputy Prime Minister) (2005) 'Vibrant local leadership', also ODPM and the Home Office (2005) 'Citizen engagement and public services: why neighbourhoods matter', both available at: www.odpm.gov.uk/localvision

Pryor, S. (2001) *The Responsible Prisoner: An Exploration of the Extent to which Imprisonment Removes Responsibility Unnecessarily and an Invitation to Change*, London: HM Prison Service.

Roberts, J. and Hough, M. (eds) (2002) *Changing Attitudes to Punishment: Public Opinion, Crime and Justice*, Cullompton: Willan Publishing.

Roberts, J. and Hough, M. (2005) 'The state of the prisons: exploring public knowledge and opinion', *Howard Journal*, vol 44, no 3, pp 286-306.

Robinson, G. (2005) 'What works in offender management?', *Howard Journal*, vol 44, no 3, pp 307-18.

SEU (Social Exclusion Unit) (2002) *Reducing Re-offending by Ex-Prisoners*, London: SEU.

Sparks, R., Bottoms, A. and Hay, W. (1996) *Prisons and the Problem of Order*, Oxford: Clarendon Press.

Tonry, M. (2004) *Punishment and Politics: Evidence and Emulation in the Making of English Crime Control Policy*, Cullompton: Willan Publishing.

Woolf, Lord (2005) 'Making sense of sentencing', available at: www.dca.gov.uk/judicial/speeches/lcj120505.htm

Zedner, L. (2004) *Criminal Justice*, Oxford: Oxford University Press.

8

Endnote

Rob Allen and Mike Hough

What would the National Offender Management Service (NOMS) have made of Frederick Rainer? He was the Hertfordshire printer who 100 years ago told the local police court magistrates that he would take an alcoholic offender under his wing and ensure that he stayed out of trouble and turned up in court. As an innovative supplier of a service, would the pioneer of the probation service have been offered a three-year contract by the Eastern Regional Offender Manager? Or would the lack of economy of scale in his work have made him uncompetitive in the new corrections market? Modern-day probation practitioners are equally uncertain about their future as the new service gets off the ground. This uncertainty was reflected in the contributions made at the colloquium on 1 July 2005.

The shape and structure of NOMS remains unclear at the time of writing, with large question marks still hanging over the likely role of the probation service. Although the Home Secretary has indicated that he means to press ahead with his plans for NOMS, it is unlikely that the role of probation in policy and practice will become clear for some considerable time. The colloquium was reminded that the Carter (2003) report had suggested the establishment of NOMS might take up to five years, so a settled picture may not be available until 2009.

At the present time, there are two distinct visions about the way work currently carried out by the probation service will be carried out under NOMS. Each was explored in the colloquium.

On the one hand, there is a vision of relatively modest change. Probation staff, employed by local probation boards – rebadged as trusts – would continue to prepare reports for courts, supervising community sentences and managing offenders released from prison. An enhanced role as offender managers (OMs) would involve continuing probation responsibility during short prison sentences. In cases of long-term imprisonment, the OM role might be taken by a prison officer. As with the traditional role of probation, OMs would know as well as manage their offenders, developing a constructive relationship to address a shared agenda of solving the problems underlying offending. In support of this work the OM could draw on a broad array of services that would help offenders sort their lives out and leave crime behind. Some services might be commissioned and organised regionally and would involve a greater role for the private and voluntary sector. But contestability would be just one tool for achieving a balanced range of programmes. Most services would be provided to offenders on the basis of their status as citizen rather than as offender. The overall response to offending would build on existing practice rather than seek to replace it. Probation would remain at the heart of the system.

A more radical vision would introduce much more of a market into the probation world. In principle all the tasks currently undertaken by probation staff might be purchased from private companies, working to large-scale contracts made with regional OMs. Offender management would not necessarily involve much human contact with the offender. The centrepiece would be the assembly and remote monitoring of programmes comprising increasingly hi-tech forms of surveillance and control. Existing probation interventions would be subject to regular market testing intended to drive up standards and ensure value for money. Local accountability would be replaced by regional performance management of contracts clearly specifying what should be provided.

These visions draw on very different themes that are to be found in the Carter (2003) report. The first sees Carter's main concern as developing a new model of offender management, to achieve a more 'seamless' system for dealing with offenders as they pass through the criminal process; while contestability could play a part in bringing this about, it is not a central element to the vision. The second sees Carter as harnessing New Public Management techniques and new technologies to 'modernise' two state bureaucracies regarded as underperforming and complacent. Contestability is central to this vision of NOMS, of course.

In this endnote we shall summarise what came out of the colloquium about the pros and cons of these competing visions, the likelihood of their coming to pass and the consequences for probation work in the future. We have not attempted to provide a statement of record. However, we hope that we have captured the flavour of the discussion.

The sentencing context

Understandably, a good deal of attention was given to the sentencing context. Probation's role and the resources available to fulfil it will in large part depend on trends in the use of prison. A relatively stable prison population in the financial year 2004-05 enabled probation boards to receive an increased budget of 10%. Increasing prison numbers in the future would put at risk the aim of matching supply and demand for places. Some colloquium participants saw Carter's target of a maximum prison population of 80,000 as a missed opportunity for a more radical policy shift away from imprisonment. The colloquium was reminded how almost two decades ago a – Conservative – Home Secretary faced with a burgeoning prison population made a positive decision to contain numbers.

At the same time there was considerable scepticism about whether the Carter strategy for containing the prison population would succeed even in keeping numbers within the 80,000 limit. The approach essentially offers sentencers enhanced sentencing options in the 2003 Criminal Justice Act (custody plus, custody minus and generic community sentence) while circumscribing their discretion through the Sentencing Guidelines Council (SGC). These sticks and carrots are to be deployed in a context in which improved effectiveness achieved by structural reforms to the prison and probation services will reduce the pool of offenders coming before the courts.

Whether sentencers will play their expected part must be an open question. Although they play a pivotal role in determining the size of the prison population, there has been minimal consultation with them over NOMS, and no serious attempt until recently to secure their 'buy-in' to the Carter vision – whether in the 'strong' or 'weak' versions that we have sketched out above. Efforts to boost sentencers' confidence in community penalties by more vigorous enforcement has already led to more offenders reaching prison through the back door of breach.

Whether they will use the new sentencing options as envisaged remains an unknown, of course, although the experience of luring sentencers away from custodial sentences by offering them tough alternatives is discouraging. A wider range of well-targeted and managed community penalties could displace short prison sentences; but on past experience in Britain and abroad, net-widening is a more likely outcome. As participants reminded the colloquium, offering courts more alternatives is not a well-attested way of limiting the use of prison.

The impact of the guidelines on judges' decision making is as yet unknown, but population pressures are likely from harsher sentences for persistent offenders and the dangerousness provisions (on which the SGC has inexplicably failed to give guidance to courts). It is discouraging that in July 2005 the Home Office published revised prison population projections because the numbers were almost 2,000 higher than the high scenario published six months earlier (Home Office, 2005). It is a brave hope that this trend will be reversed within a three- or five-year period by reductions in the pool of offenders coming before the courts achieved by improved NOMS performance in rehabilitating offenders. Any assessment of the contribution of a corrections system to crime control has to take account of the very limited reach of the formal criminal justice system into offending, and the very low detection rates that are achieved for most crimes.

The reintroduction of probation liaison arrangements with sentencers was felt to be important but a constantly changing cast of service providers, organised in 10 regions, could be less responsive to local courts than the current 42 probation areas. Unless courts have greater confidence in community sentences, rising prison numbers will account for an ever-increasing proportion of the NOMS budget.

If an improved infrastructure of services for offenders succeeds in reducing re-offending, the number of candidates for custody could fall. The two mechanisms by which NOMS is seeking to achieve this goal are improved case management and more effective programmes improved by contestability.

Offender management

The aim of a seamless response to offenders leaving prison is perhaps the least controversial element in the NOMS proposals. Despite the danger that eroding the distinction between prison and community supervision could make imprisonment appear an almost routine form of offender management rather than the severest sanction our democracy can apply to its citizens, the idea that prisoners should serve their sentences close to home and that interventions should be planned and organised 'through the gate' seems unarguable. There was nonetheless uncertainty about whether the NOMS case management model would achieve improvements in the day-to-day interactions between probation officer and offender. Contributors pointed to some inherent contradictions – between the continuity of 'one offender, one manager' on the one hand and the fragmentation inherent in separating interventions from management, on the other. Voluntary organisations welcomed the spirit of the aims but felt reality on the ground was a world away from the aspiration. Proponents of the approach pointed to the positives to emerge from the North West Pathfinder: both offenders and staff appear to like the 'through the gate' approach (PA Consultancy Group and MORI, 2005).

The question remained whether 'seamlessness' could be achieved without the wholesale upheaval involved in creating a new organisation, or rather, a new network of organisations. For many at the colloquium, continuing to build up the necessary skills in the existing probation workforce – insight, empathy, pro-social modelling and problem solving – would be a preferable focus of energy and resources than large-scale structural reform.

There was scepticism too about what contestability had to offer in this area. While NOMS is often described as a merger or integration of probation and prisons, it is seen by some as the opposite. Splitting up services on the purchaser–provider model could divide the probation world into new and different silos. Despite the rhetoric about joining up, additional fragmentation is likely if service providers need to keep their competitive edge in a market environment. The most recent Inspectorate of Prisons' report on the Wolds (HMIP, 2005), the first private prison in Europe, found that 13 years after its establishment, it was still not part of the area resettlement strategy, did not use OASys (the national offender assessment system) and did not apply safer custody procedures.

Contestability

The colloquium revealed more fundamental unease about contestability in probation. While privatisation had been introduced into prison to address particular problems – disturbances, staff unrest, weak management and poor regimes – it was not clear to all what contestability in probation was for. As one contributor put it: 'Radical surgery as applied to prisons is not necessary for a probation service whose main problems arise from poor nutrition and lack of continuity of care'. The national probation service had been in existence for just two years when NOMS was announced and its performance has been improving steadily.

Some suggested that contestability was only one aspect of the NOMS proposals – a device for injecting a little creative tension into the system that was not intended to shift probation from its central position. In the words of one participant, contestability was never intended to be more than 'one piece of the jigsaw'. However, others pointed out that in at least one of the purchaser provider models being considered at that time by government, there was no guarantee that a probation board in a particular area would survive if it did not win enough business. They questioned the idea that contestability could in practice be contained to the margins of probation organisation: large private sector organisations would only be tempted into this marketplace if there were substantial opportunities for them. And leaving aside issues of practicability, some participants saw the NOMS proposals to create opportunities for new providers as the application to criminal justice of the New Public Management formula across the public sector to which the Treasury and the Cabinet Office were deeply attached – whatever the Home Office and other criminal justice departments might think.

Some participants felt that this would be no bad thing, arguing that much of the 'public good, private bad' feeling in public services merely reflected producer interest. Monopoly provision of public services by state bureaucracies could hardly lay claim to an impressive track record. Universal education's failure to teach millions of children to read or write had demanded radical reforms. So too failures in offender rehabilitation suggested that a new approach was needed.

The experience of prisons privatisation provided the colloquium with an interesting but inexact parallel. The best of private prisons appear to outperform public prisons in some aspects of the quality of prisoner treatment, and the worst do rather worse. (The precise picture is not entirely clear, however, because commercial confidentiality means not all learning enters the public domain.) However, the prison service faced very different challenges 15 years ago from the probation service today. The Home Office and senior managers had to deal with a substantially disaffected, uncooperative workforce whose values hardly exemplified public service values and the spirit of altruism. The threat of privatisation may well have generated precisely the tension that was needed within the system to achieve some improvements in the treatment of prisoners – although this might have been achieved in other ways.

As participants pointed out, the government is grappling with a very different problem in probation – a service whose commitment to the welfare of offenders is seen to stand in the way of the introduction of a form of probation work that places more emphasis on the control of risk. Whether the tensions of contestability offer the smoothest or most certain route to this end is unclear. Certainly the strengths of the private prisons seem to lie not in their ability to control risk but in the quality of their treatment of prisoners. In the case of probation, privatisation could be the right solution to the wrong problem.

The question whether there were distinctive public service values to be found within existing probation providers emerged as a significant bone of contention. Some argued that beneath the surface, there was little to distinguish between the value systems of commercial, public and voluntary sector bodies. According to this perspective, the private sector was just as capable as the public and not-for-profit sectors of treating offenders with dignity and respect, and they could be held to doing so through well-specified contracts. The opposing view, of course, was that the profit motive sits uneasily with the commitment to helping others that is an essential component of effective work with offenders. A narrower – but no less important – point is whether the integrity of court reports could be threatened under a contestability regime in which those who produce Pre-Sentence Reports have a commercial interest in the outcome. (Once contestability is in place, this problem could emerge regardless of whether the reports in question are prepared by staff of a commercial enterprise or by probation officers.)

Some discussion was given to the role of the voluntary sector, which can offer probation work not only that commitment to helping others but flexibility and a capacity for innovation. Various risks faced the voluntary sector under NOMS. Small local organisations might be disadvantaged in competing for contracts against the larger national charities, which are better resourced to bid for work, and better placed to establish alliances with private sector organisations. There was also thought to be a risk that the strengths of the voluntary sector could be progressively eroded by exposure to the marketplace. The more that they have to engage in competition for government contracts, the more one would expect them to adopt the perspectives and values of the private sector, and lose those distinctive characteristics for which they are valued.

The governance of work with offenders

The colloqium ended with a discussion of the governance of probation work under NOMS. One set of arguments, relatively little heard, relates to the fundamentally local nature of probation work, and its links with wider social policy initiatives to tackle exclusion, regenerate communities and renew civil society. As with much of government policy, the NOMS proposals were thought to demonstrate an unresolved tension between a commitment to localism and to civil renewal, on the one hand, and to a 'command and control' approach to reform on the other. The dilemma facing a government eager for rapid improvement in public services is that, however attractive it might be in principle, the civil renewal agenda will take years to achieve. Centrally driven root-and-branch reform – if it can be achieved – fits within electoral time frames even if it is less than fully compatible with the civil renewal agenda.

Many participants were clearly attracted to the vision of a probation and prison system with strong local roots and local accountability, drawing on the strengths of local communities and local organisations. It was possible to envisage ways in which contestability could be used in a creative way, to draw both voluntary sector and private organisations into probation work at local level, in a spirit of equal partnership engaged on a shared enterprise. But it was more realistic to expect the evolution of a form of contract culture in probation work in which commercial competition fostered distrust and fragmentation between large consortia of providers with little investment in, or commitment to, local communities.

Conclusions

What seems clearer is that if it is to survive and flourish, the probation service cannot afford to be complacent, needing to take a long hard look at its strengths and weaknesses with a view to proposing ways to reform itself. It needs to make the case for exceptionalism – that the nature of its work, its size and its complex relationships with other agencies make it unsuitable for the full rigours of the New Public Management orthodoxy.

Our own view is that there is a clear case to be made that work with offenders has distinctive qualities to it that militate against the wholesale implementation of 'marketplace' reforms. As was clear from the proceedings of the colloquium, there are unresolved questions about the importance that should be attached to the 'public service' values that are to be found in the best of probation of work – and in voluntary bodies. There are questions about the importance that should be attached to the institutional legitimacy to which the probation service can lay claim. There are the attractions of a genuinely local network of local services, with a local as well as a national identity, and with local systems of accountability. A great deal more work – and consultation – is needed to find the best way of engineering a system that successfully addresses both local and national interests.

The solutions currently under development are certainly not the only ones. There are other options besides structuring accountability nationally or regionally. One possibility is for work with offenders to be organised at a radically more local level, working with local authorities whose responsibilities for housing, education and social care make them crucial partners in the enterprise. Nor is this simply a pipe dream. It is the route that is being taken in Scotland. After a full and proper process of consultation, initial government plans for a NOMS-style correctional agency were replaced by a system of community justice authorities building on local not central government traditions.

South of the border, the government did not allow a period of consultation, reflection and debate following the publication of Lord Carter's (2003) report. Had such discussions taken place, much of the divisive and morale-sapping controversy that has dogged NOMS might have been avoided. Yet it is to be hoped that the chapters in this book and the discussions at the colloquium will feed into the debates to come over the coming months and years.

References
Carter, P. (2003) *Managing Offenders, Reducing Crime: A New Approach*, London: Prime Minister's Strategy Unit.

HMIP (HM Inspectorate of Prisons) (2005) *Report on a Full Announced Inspection of HMP Wolds 15-19 November 2004*, London: Home Office.

Home Office (2005) *Updated and Revised Prison Population Projections 2005-2011 England and Wales*, Statistical Bulletin 10/15, London: Home Office.

PA Consultancy Group and MORI (2005) *Action Research Study of the Implementation of the National Offender Management Model in the North West Pathfinder*, Home Office Online Report 32/05, London: Home Office.

Also available from The Policy Press

Youth crime and youth justice
Public opinion in England and Wales
Mike Hough and Julian V. Roberts

This report presents the findings from the first national, representative survey of public attitudes to youth crime and youth justice in England and Wales. It carries clear policy implications in relation to both public education and reform of the youth justice system.

Paperback £14.99 ISBN 1 86134 649 2
245 x 170mm 80 pages November 2004

From dependency to work
Addressing the multiple needs of offenders with drug problems
Tim McSweeney, Victoria Herrington, Mike Hough, Paul J. Turnbull and Jim Parsons

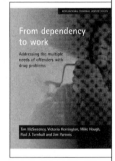

This report presents the findings from one of the first evaluations of a British programme to integrate drug and alcohol treatment with mental health services, and education, training and employment support – the 'From Dependency to Work (D2W)' programme. It provides an invaluable insight into the challenges and difficulties of integrating services in this way and highlights important lessons for central and regional government on funding and working with the voluntary sector to deliver services.

Paperback £14.99 ISBN 1 86134 660 3
245 x 170mm 88 pages December 2004

Plural policing
The mixed economy of visible patrols in England and Wales
Adam Crawford, Stuart Lister, Sarah Blackburn and Jonathan Burnett

This timely and important report draws together the findings of an extensive two-year study of developments in the provision of visible policing in England and Wales. Exploring the dynamic relations between different public and private providers, it combines an overview of national developments with a detailed analysis of six focused case studies, including two city centres, one out-of-town shopping centre, an industrial park and two residential areas.

Paperback £14.99 ISBN 1 86134 671 9
245 x 170mm 128 pages March 2005

Integrating victims in restorative youth justice
Adam Crawford and Tom Burden

It is a key aim of current youth justice policy to introduce principles of restorative justice and involve victims in responses to crime. This is most evident in the referral order and youth offender panels established by the Youth Justice and Criminal Evidence Act 1999. However, the challenges involved in delivering a form of restorative youth justice that is sensitive to the needs of victims are considerable. This report provides an illuminating evaluation of the manner in which one Youth Offending Service sought to integrate victims into the referral order process.

Paperback £14.99 ISBN 1 86134 785 5
245 x 170mm 120 pages November 2005

To order further copies of this publication or any other Policy Press titles please visit **www.policypress.org.uk** or contact:

In the UK and Europe:
Marston Book Services, PO Box 269, Abingdon, Oxon,
OX14 4YN, UK
Tel: +44 (0)1235 465500
Fax: +44 (0)1235 465556
Email: direct.orders@marston.co.uk

In the USA and Canada:
ISBS, 920 NE 58th Street, Suite 300, Portland, OR 97213-3786, USA
Tel: +1 800 944 6190 (toll free)
Fax: +1 503 280 8832
Email: info@isbs.com

In Australia and New Zealand:
DA Information Services, 648 Whitehorse Road Mitcham,
Victoria 3132, Australia
Tel: +61 (3) 9210 7777
Fax: +61 (3) 9210 7788
E-mail: service@dadirect.com.au

Further information about all of our titles can be found on our website.